The Collected Lute Music
of
JOHN DOWLAND

The Collected Lute Music
of
JOHN DOWLAND

transcribed and edited

by

DIANA POULTON

and

BASIL LAM

THIRD EDITION

FABER *ff* MUSIC

© 1974, 1978, 1981 by Faber Music Ltd
First published in 1974 by Faber Music Ltd
in association with Faber & Faber Ltd
This edition published in 1981 by Faber Music Ltd
3 Queen Square London WC1N 3AU
Reprinted in 1995
Music drawn by Jonathan Barkwith
Printed in England by Caligraving Ltd
All rights reserved

ISBN 0-571-10039-2

The cover illustration is *The Lute Player*,
by Bartolomeo Veneto, *fl*.1502–1530

To buy Faber Music publications or to find out about the full range of titles available
please contact your local music retailer or Faber Music sales enquiries:

Faber Music Limited, Burnt Mill, Elizabeth Way, Harlow, CM20 2HX England
Tel: +44 (0)1279 82 89 82   Fax: +44 (0)1279 82 89 83
sales@fabermusic.com   www.fabermusic.com

CONTENTS

INTRODUCTION

During his lifetime John Dowland was one of the few English composers whose fame spread throughout Europe. He has never been entirely forgotten although his music was almost completely ignored during the whole of the eighteenth century and most of the nineteenth. The early twentieth century saw a dawning recognition among scholars and specialists of the rare quality of his work. In the nineteen twenties the appearance of the song books, edited by Dr. E. H. Fellowes, made this aspect of his work available, and his greatness as a song writer is well established. It was not, however, until the revival of an appreciation of the lute as an important instrument in its own right, that opportunities to hear Dowland's lute music began to appear outside the small circle of devotees of early music. A certain number of Dowland's compositions for the lute are becoming known, but there is still a large proportion which has remained shrouded in the obscurity of the original manuscripts and many fine works have not yet been taken into the general repertoire. With this edition, as complete as the editors have been able to make it, it is hoped that a wider knowledge of his music will be achieved, so that his greatness in this field also will gain general acknowledgement.

In the preparation of this book the editors have received much generous and valuable help. In particular they wish to express their thanks to the Gulbenkian Foundation whose grant of financial help made it possible to continue the work at a time when it seemed that circumstances might force it to be abandoned; to a generous friend, who wishes to remain anonymous, who also contributed financial help; to Desmond Dupré, who helped with proof reading, and who made many useful suggestions; to Richard Newton whose great knowledge of English lute music helped to solve many problems; to General Prynne who allowed unlimited use of his microfilms; to Robert Spencer for making available the Tollemache MS for study, and for granting permission to include works from this and the Mynshall MS, both of which are now in his possession. Acknowledgement is also gladly extended to all those libraries which have allowed extracts from their MSS and books to be included in this volume.

D.P.

B.R.L.

The prolonged and laborious task of assembling, codifying and transcribing the material must be credited to my co-editor, my part being in the main confined to help both in the preparation of the final text and the making of the version in staff notation.

B.R.L.

*CALENDAR OF DATES IN THE LIFE OF JOHN DOWLAND

1563		Year of birth.
1580		Goes to Paris in the service of Sir Henry Cobham, Ambassador to the French Court.
1584		Is sent on a mission by Sir Edward Stafford (who succeeded Cobham as Ambassador) on behalf of some English merchants imprisoned in France and condemned to the galleys.
1586		Probably returned to England during this year.
1588	July 8th	Is admitted Mus.Bac from Christ Church, Oxford. In *Apologia Musices* is mentioned by Dr. John Case among the most famous musicians of his day.
1590	November 17th	"His golden locks" sung by Robert Hales at the Tiltyard, Westminster, at the Accession Day celebrations.
1592		"My heart and tongue were twins" sung before the Queen at Sudeley Castle. Six harmonizations contributed to Est's *Whole Booke of Psalmes*.
1594		His application for a post at Court being rejected he leaves England with a permit to travel abroad signed by Sir Robert Cecil and the Earl of Essex. He visits the Duke of Brunswick and the Landgrave of Hesse, then travels south with the intention of visiting Luca Marenzio in Rome. He plays before the Grand Duke of Tuscany in Florence, but leaves the city hurriedly when exiled English Catholics living there attempt to involve him in a plot against the Queen. He returns to Germany.
1595	November 10th	From Nuremberg he writes a detailed account of his journey and of the activities of the exiles to Sir Robert Cecil.
1596		Returns to the Landgrave's Court sometime during this year. Seven of Dowland's compositions appear in Barley's *New Booke of Tabliture* without the composer's permission; "false and unperfect".
	December 1st	Letter written by Henry Noel to Dowland urging his return home in the likelihood of the Queen's granting him a post at Court.
1596-7	February 26th	Death of Henry Noel. "Lamentatio Henrici Noel" composed for the funeral in Westminster Abbey.
1597	October 21st	*The First Booke of Songes* entered in the Stationers' Register. Dowland describes himself on the title-page as "Bacheler of Musicke in both the Universities".
	November 21st	Giles Farnaby's *Canzonets to fowr voyces* entered in the Stationers' Register. Dated 1598 it contains a commendatory poem by Dowland.

*A note on the Calendar

England continued to use the "Old Style" calendar until the beginning of 1752, with the year starting on March 25th. Most Continental countries, including Denmark, adopted the Gregorian reforms in 1582 or soon after. With the "New Style" calendar the year commenced on January 1st and the date was advanced by ten days in order to compensate for the accumulated error of the old way of reckoning.

In the above list of the main events in Dowland's life all dates from Danish and other Continental sources are given in the "New Style", while happenings in England are referred to in the "Old".

With the dating of letters from Englishmen abroad it is often impossible to be sure which system was in use.

1598	February 9th	Letter written to Dowland by the Langrave of Hesse offering him a post at the Landgrave's Court.
	July 16th	Appointment offered at the Court of Christian IV of Denmark. In Richard Barnfield's Poems: *In divers humors* he is commended in the well-known sonnet "If music and sweet poetry agree".
	November 18th	Dowland begins his duties as royal lutenist at the Danish Court with a salary of 500 daler a year, payment beginning from that date. Francis Meres pays tribute to his genius in *Palladis Tamia*, printed during this year.
1599		Dowland writes commendatory poem for Richard Alison's *The Psalmes of David in Meter*.
1600	July 15th	*The Second Booke of Songes* entered in the Stationers' Register. The epistle is dated "From Helsignoure in Denmark the first of June 1600". George Eastland buys the MS from Mrs. Dowland for £20 and half the expected reward from Lucy Countess of Bedford for the dedication.
	July 28th	Dowland signs a receipt for 600 daler in excess of his salary, paid him on the instruction of the Court Treasurer. He returns to England during the latter part of the year to buy instruments and engage other musicians for the Danish Court. Reprint of *The First Booke of Songes*.
1601	February 5th	The Danish Customs receive a letter saying they will be repaid the 300 daler they advanced to Dowland for buying instruments in England.
	June 6th	Dowland receives a present from the Danish King of a portrait of His Royal Majesty in "plain gold".
	September 5th	The Customs in Elsinore receive another letter assuring them that the 300 daler advanced to Dowland will be repaid.
1603	February 19th	Salary paid in Denmark and then entries in the Royal Accounts cease until July 10th, 1604.
1602-3	February 21st	*The Third and Last Booke of Songes* entered in the Stationers' Register. The greater part of this year appears to have been spent away from Denmark.
	September 20th to October 4th	The plague rages in London all through the summer and the King and Queen leave London to escape the contagion. Before returning to town in the autumn they visit Winchester where a masque is presented for Prince Henry. Dowland "has access" to Her Majesty while she is in this city, possibly soliciting a post at Court. Second reprint of *The First Booke of Songes*.
1604	April 2nd	*Lachrimae or Seaven Teares* entered in the Stationers' Register. By this date Dowland occupies a house in Fetter Lane.
	July 10th	He has apparently returned to Denmark as he is paid a year's salary in arrears.
1605		All through this year he is beset with money troubles and draws his salary in advance.
1606	March 10th	He is dismissed from the Court of Denmark while the King is absent on a visit to the Duke of Brunswick. Third reprint of *The First Booke of Songes*.
1608		Fourth reprint of *The First Booke of Songes*?
1608-9	January 20th	Dowland's translation of the *Micrologus* of Ornithoparcus is entered in the Stationers' Register.
1610		*Varietie of Lute-Lessons* printed, containing nine pieces by Dowland, a translation of "Necessarie Observations belonging to Lute-playing" by Besardus, and Dowland's own "Other Necessary Observations belonging to the Lute". *A Musicall Banquet* is printed, containing three songs by Dowland.
1611	August 9th	Henry Peacham's *Minerva Britanna* entered in the Stationers' Register; printed 1612. It contains the poem "Here, Philomel in silence sits alone" addressed "Ad amicum suum Iohannes Doulandum".

	October 28th	*A Pilgrimes Solace* entered in the Stationers' Register. Printed 1612. Dowland is now lutenist to Lord Walden.
1612	October 28th	Appointed one of the Lutes to James I, in the place of Richard Pyke (died May 21st, 1568), at the salary of 20d pence a day.
1613		Final reprint of *The First Booke of Songes*.
1613-14	January 27th	Sir William Leighton's *Teares or Lamentacions of a sorrowfull soule* entered in Stationers' Register. Printed 1614. Contains two sacred songs by Dowland and a commendatory poem from his pen.
	February	Plays the lute in Chapman's "Masque of the Inner Temple and Lincoln's Inn" at Whitehall during the festivities connected with the marriage of Princess Elizabeth on February 14th. Robert Johnson receives £45 for writing songs and music, Dowland is paid £2 10s. od. for playing.
1614		Dowland contributes a poem "in commendation of this *worke*" to Thomas Ravenscroft's *A Briefe Discourse*.
1621		He contributes a new setting of Psalm 100 to Thomas Ravenscroft's *Whole Booke of Psalmes*. For the first time he is styled Dr. John Dowland.
1622		Thomas Tomkins in *Songs of 3, 4, 5 and 6 parts* dedicates the seventh song to "Doctor Douland". This style is also used in the Audit office Accounts from this year onwards.
1624		Dowland is named with Byrd, Bull, Morley and "the rest of our rare Artists", by William Webb in a poem in Francis Pilkington's *Second set of Madrigals*.
1625-6	January 20th	Receives his final payment and is succeeded in his post at Court by his son Robert (by letters under the signet 26, April 2nd, Chas. I).
	February 20th	The name "John Dowland Doctor of Musicke" is entered in the Burial Register of St. Anne, Blackfriars.

BIOGRAPHICAL NOTES

8 and 19. CAPTAIN DIGORIE PIPER (1559–1590). Member of a land-owning family of some standing in Launceston, Cornwall. In 1585 the *Sweepstake* of London was put to sea under a Commission of Reprisal granted by the High Court of Admiralty to attack shipping belonging to subjects of the King of Spain. Digorie Piper was Captain. During the next few months, however, instead of confining his attentions to Spanish vessels, Piper attacked and spoiled a number of French, Dutch, Flemish and Danish boats going about their lawful business up and down the Channel. On June 10th, 1586, he was charged with piracy before Mr. Justice Caesar and made a full confession. He apparently escaped hanging as he lived until 1590 and was buried in his own parish on January 20th of that year.

11. BRIGIDE FLEETWOOD, daughter of Thomas Fleetwood, Esq., of The Vache, Chalfont St. Giles, Master of the Mint and Sheriff of the County of Buckinghamshire in 1564. She married, in December 1589, Sir William Smith, nephew and heir of Sir Thomas Smith, Principal Secretary of State to Edward VI and Elizabeth. The family seat was Hill Hall, Theydon Mount, Essex. She was related by marriage to Katherine Darcy (*see* No. 24).

12. DR. JOHN CASE (?–1600). Became a Fellow of St. John's College, Oxford, in 1572 but later left his Fellowship and married. He became a Doctor of Medicine in 1589 and built up a successful practise. He wrote a number of books on various aspects of Aristotle's writings and also *Apologia Musices* (1588) in which Dowland is mentioned as among the most famous composers of his time. *The Praise of Musicke* (1586) is also attributed to him. His name is perpetuated in a six-part setting by William Byrd of a poem by Thomas Watson, known as "A Gratifications unto Master John Case . . .".

14, 14a, SIR JOHN LANGTON (1560–1616), of Langton in Lincolnshire. Educated at Magdalen
and 33. College, Oxford. Entered Lincoln's Inn as a student in 1579. Knighted by James I in 1603 and became High Sheriff of Leicestershire in 1612.

17. LADY RUSSELL (1528–1609). Almost certainly Elizabeth, Lady Russell, one of the five daughters of Sir Anthony Cooke of Gidea Hall, Essex. These sisters were considered to be among the most learned women of their time. One, Mildred, became the wife of William Cecil, Lord Burleigh; another, Ann, married Sir Nicholas Bacon. Elizabeth married first Sir Thomas Hoby, translator of Castiglione's *The Booke of the Courtier* (1561). After his death she married in 1574, John Lord Russell, son and heir to the Duke of Bedford. She was one of the signatories to the petitions to the Privy Council from the residents within the precincts of Blackfriars, which, in 1596, sought to have James Burbage restrained from opening "a common playhouse" in the old friary building.

24, 41, 45 KATHERINE DARCY or Darcie. Daughter and heiress of Sir Henry Darcy. On June 25th,
and 53 1591, she married Gervase Clifton, son of Sir John Clifton of Barrington Court, Somerset. Clifton was knighted sometime before 1597 and created a peer in 1608. Joan or Jane Clifton, sister of Gervase, married Sir William Fleetwood, Brigide's eldest brother.

26. SIR JOHN SOUCH, son of Sir John Souch of Codnor Castle, Derbyshire. He studied at Trinity College, Oxford; was admitted to Gray's Inn in 1582; knighted April 23rd, 1603. Dowland's *Third and Last Booke of Songs* was also dedicated to him.

29. GILES HOBY (*d.* 1626), either the half-brother or son of the half-brother of Sir Thomas Hoby, first husband of Lady Russell.

32 and MRS. VAUX. Probably Elizabeth Roper, wife of George, eldest son of William Lord Vaux
57. of Harrowden.

36. MR. KNIGHT. Identification impossible.

37. THE LORD CHAMBERLAIN at the time of the publication of this piece was George Carey, second Baron Hunsdon (1547–1603), son of Henry Carey, first Baron Hunsdon, a cousin of Queen Elizabeth's. He succeeded to the title on the death of his father in 1596 and was appointed Lord Chamberlain of the Household in March, 1597.

38. THE LORD VISCOUNT LISLE (1563–1626). Robert Sidney, son of Sir Henry Sidney and brother of Sir Philip Sidney. Member of Parliament and distinguished soldier, he was knighted by the Earl of Leicester in 1586, while serving in the Wars of the Low Countries. He became Chamberlain to the Queen, Anne of Denmark in 1603; created Viscount Lisle in 1605; and in 1618, the Earldom of Leicester was revived in his favour. Robert Jones's *Second Book of Songs* (1601) is dedicated to him.

40. CHRISTIAN IV, King of Denmark (reigned 1588–1648, crowned 1596), in whose service Dowland spent the years from November 18th, 1598, to March 10th, 1606. Christian was a discriminating patron of music and the arts, though singularly unsuccessful in war. Contemporary accounts stress his excessive propensity to drunkenness.

41. QUEEN ELIZABETH I (*b.* 1553, reigned 1588–1603). It would be superfluous to give biographical details here but to the extent to which her life touched upon that of Dowland, it is perhaps worth saying that his expressed belief that his Catholicism prevented his securing an appointment at her Court does not accord either with her known attitude towards Catholics or with the facts of Dowland's own life. Dowland dedicated no music to her until after her death.

42a. ROBERT DEVEREUX, second Earl of Essex (1567–1601). The history of the Earl of Essex, his rise to power as favourite of Queen Elizabeth, his rebellion, disgrace and execution in 1601 are too well-known to call for repetition here.

43. LADY RICH (*b.* 1562 or 1563). Penelope Devereux, elder sister of Robert, Earl of Essex, was, after her father's death, married against her will, by her guardians, to Lord Rich. Later she left Lord Rich and joined Charles Blount, Lord Mountjoy. Divorced in 1605, she married Blount, by that time created Earl of Devonshire. She was the "Stella" of Sir Philip Sidney's *Astrophel and Stella*.

44 and
44a. FERDINANDO STANLEY, fifth Earl of Derby (1559–1594). He traced his descent from Henry VII through Mary, Queen Dowager of France, sister of Henry VIII, and her second husband Charles Brandon, Duke of Suffolk. On account of this position in the line of succession some attempt was made by the Catholic faction to involve him in a claim to the throne, but he refused to become entangled in any such dangerous adventures. He was a great patron of the arts and several books were dedicated to him. As Lord Strange he was, for several years, patron of a company of actors which was known by his name. He succeeded to the Earldom of Derby on the death of his father together with other dignities and titles which included sovereignty of the Isle of Man.

47. Possibly the same SIR JOHN SMITH of Hough in Cheshire, to whom Pilkington dedicated his *Second Set of Madrigals* (1624), but William A. Shaw in *The Knights of England* gives a John Smith of Essex, who was knighted at Royston in 1605. This would agree very well with his being plain "mr Smythe" in **FD** and Sir John Smith in **Var.**

48 and
48a. LADY LAITON. Probably Winifred, daughter of Simon Harcourt of Ellenhall in Staffordshire, wife of Sir William Leighton, poet and composer, best known for his *Teares or Lamentations of a Sorrowfull Soule* (1613 and 1614).

50 and
56. MRS. WHITE. Possibly Anne Cecil (sister of William Cecil, Lord Burleigh, 1520–1598), who married Thomas White of Tuxford, Nottinghamshire.

54. LADY HUNSDON. Elizabeth, second daughter of Sir John Spenser of Althorp, Northamptonshire and wife of George Carey, second Lord Hunsdon. She was a noted patroness of letters. Her elder sister Alice, married as her first husband Ferdinando Earl of Derby.

55. The WINTERS were related to the Vaux family by marriage and to the Treshams. It was from among these Catholic families of the Midlands that those taking part in the Gunpowder Plot were largely drawn. This Mrs. Winter could have been Jean or Jane Ingleby who married George Winter and became the mother of Robert and Thomas Winter, two of the leading conspirators.

59. RICHARD TARLETON (*d.* 1588). Famous comic actor. He is credited with the authorship of *News out of Purgatory* and a number of ballads and songs. He died in poverty.

65. LORD STRANG. Probably Lord Strange, the title borne by Ferdinando Stanley until he

succeeded to the Earldom of Derby in 1593. *See* No. 44.

66.   Lord Willoughby. Peregrine Bertie, eleventh Baron Willoughby de Eresby (1555–1601) was the son of Katherine, third wife of Charles Brandon Duke of Suffolk. After the death of the Duke she married an obscure gentleman named Richard Bertie. Their son Peregrine became a distinguished soldier and in 1587 was appointed Commander of the English forces in the Netherlands in place of the Earl of Leicester.

THE TRANSCRIPTIONS

Although tablature has a distinct advantage for the lutenist over staff notation, it has the weakness of being unable to convey the precise movement of the individual parts in a musical composition. In other words, tablature, though indicating where any given note begins is unable to show, except where another note falls on the same string, where that note ends. Thus the elucidation of the harmonic structure and the counterpoint devolves upon the performer, or, in the case of transcriptions into staff notation, upon the editor.

The most skilful among the lutenist composers acquired a remarkable ability to suggest a great deal more than the hand can actually perform on the instrument. A well-written passage, played by a good performer, will suggest the presence of several complete parts, while in fact, owing to the exigencies of lute technique, the player is unable, from time to time, to maintain some of the notes required by the harmony and counterpoint. The editors, therefore, in the transcriptions, while avoiding as far as possible, the prolonging of notes in such a way as to be impracticable on the lute, have found it necessary, from time to time, in order to give a coherent account of the music, to show a note as held, even though it may be beyond the technical limitations of the lute. In certain cases, in order to make this clear, the duration beyond which a note cannot be sustained is shown by the use of a tie and a bracket, *e.g.* ♩[♩] . Thus it is hoped that the staff notation, while making the music available to a wider circle, will also serve as an aid to the lutenist in understanding the full implications of the tablature.

The occurrence of hemiola rhythm, so ambiguous even in the staff notation of the Baroque music, is not infrequent in galliards. The interpretation of these ambiguities is conjectural, due attention having been given to the harmonic sense, though even here opinion may differ.

To make clear precisely what has been done in these transcriptions the following summary of points should be noted:

1. Any note added to the original text, either conjecturally or from another source, is placed in square brackets. No further mention is made of these additions.
2. Editorial emendations are marked by numbered footnotes, which give the original reading.
3. Where bar lines have been regularized, unless otherwise mentioned, the position of the original bar is shown by an asterisk over the transcription.
4. Where absent, double bars have been added to the end of strains and repeats.
5. Repeat marks have been added where definite marking is found in the sources. These markings may be either a figure 2 placed over the double bar; the sign ·5 ; or a double bar with dots. In a few instances the latter marks are used purely decoratively and in such cases they have been ignored.
6. Time values have been halved except in the cases of 47, 47a, 48, 52, 61, 62, 63, 66 and 66a, where it was felt the music was better expressed by retaining the original values.
7. Inconsistency is often found in the use of the time mark | . In some sources it represents two beats, in others four. In this edition, except in the pieces already mentioned, ₵ is used to represent a minim, while | represents a semibreve.
8. A note stemmed at the top and bottom with a bracket round one stem indicates that one note only in the tablature represents two voices.
9. Unless there is any ambiguity accidentals apply only to the bar and the particular voice to which they are added. They are not subsequently corrected.

10. In each case a single source has been followed. Important differences of reading in other texts are given in the Notes.
11. Ornament signs have been included in the tablature as accurately as possible wherever they occur in the sources. They have not, however, been transferred to the staff notation since, in many cases, there is room for difference of opinion as to which note the sign is intended to govern and of the manner in which the signs themselves are to be interpreted.
12. Fermata signs, often placed over the final chord instead of a time mark, or over the final double bar, have been omitted.
13. The vertical lines, drawn from letters on the upper lines of the tablature stave to those on the lower ones, or used to fill the spaces between the letters of a chord, have been omitted. Their function is as a visual aid, of particular use in MS where the letters can easily be written out of true alignment. They are seldom found in printed lute music since the more accurate placing of the tablature letters in the printer's forme made their use unnecessary.

The Sources

Special difficulties surround any attempt to make a collected edition of Dowland's lute music for he left no convenient printed edition of his complete solo works such as he did with the song books, and the pieces have to be gathered together from the most diverse sources; sources which are scattered throughout the libraries and museums of England, Ireland, Scotland, Wales, America and the Continent of Europe, and which, moreover, vary enormously in the reliability of the texts.

Unfortunately, for some reason which is not clear, England lagged behind the Continent in the production of printed collections of solo lute music, although the printed song books of the English lutenist composers are excellent examples of music printing. Three of Dowland's pieces are printed in his own song books, one in Robert Dowland's *Musicall Banquet*, nine are in *Varietie of Lute-Lessons* and seven in William Barley's *Newe Booke of Tabliture*. These latter Dowland himself described as "false and unperfect". For the rest it is to the great MS collections that contain hundreds of pieces by all the well-known English composers, and numerous foreign ones as well, that the editor must turn for the majority of Dowland's works.

1. A Fantasie

(1) **d** on 2 (2) **d** on 6 (3) **ʈ** on 5 added (4) **ε** on 5 added.

(5) **d** on 6 (6) Time mark three notes earlier (7) **d** on 1 for **d** on 2 (8) **b** on 4 (9) **ε** on 6 (10) **ε** on 6.

(11) d on 3.

(12) d on 5 (13) d on 6 (14) ε on 1 from **38**.

6

(15) Bar missing—supplied from No. 1a and 30 (16) ♩ on 6 (17) ♩ on 5 added in original. Reading follows **JP., G.** and No. 1a.

1a. A Fantasie

(2) Two beats, present in all other versions, have been eliminated at this point.

(3) Seven bars, present in all earlier versions, have been eliminated at this point. See No. 1.

(4) ε on 1.

(7) **d** on I.

2. Forlorn Hope Fancy

(1) **τ** on 5. Reading follows **MHM.**

(2) Written **τ** on 5 one crotchet earlier.

(3) (4)

(5) (6)

(7)

(3) Ɛ on 5 (4) Ɛ on 6 (5) ᴜ on 5 (6) ᴅ on 2. These two corrections follow **MHM.** (7) Bar line missing.

3. Farewell

(1) Bar lines misplaced by two beats until the end.

4. Farewell
(An "In Nomine")

(1) τ on 5.

† This note cannot, of course, be held on the lute.

† See note to bar 31.

† See note to bar 31 (2) **d** on 3 (3) **r** on 2 (4) **r** on 1.

5. A Fancy

(1) ♭♭a on 3 (2) ♭ on 4.

6. A Fancy

(1)

[10]

(1) **d** on 3 placed under **ᵹ** on 1 (2) Bar line placed two beats later.

(2)

(3) Bar line omitted (4) Bar line omitted (5) Bar lines misplaced by two beats until bar 19 (6) ʈ on 6 placed under ∂ on 1 (7) ∂ on 6.

(8) τ on 4 (9) Bar lines misplaced by two beats until the end (10) Three letters from **D9**.

(11) ♭ on 5 (12) Bar line omitted (13) ℰ on 6 (14) ℰ on 2 (15) τ on 1.

7. A Fancy

(2) Time marks are 𝄐

8. Piper's Pavan

For Galliard see p. 85.

(1) ꞇ on 5 instead of ꝺ on 4.

9. Semper Dowland Semper Dolens

(1) 𝄽 on 1, ♪ on 2, ♪ on 3 (2) ♩ on 1, ♭ on 2 (3) 𝄽 on 6 one quaver later.

(4) ℰ on 3 for ℰ on 4 (5) **ᵭ** on 4 added (6) From **JP** and **W** (7) Bar line misplaced.

(8) **d** on 1 (9) **d** on 2.

10. Solus Cum Sola

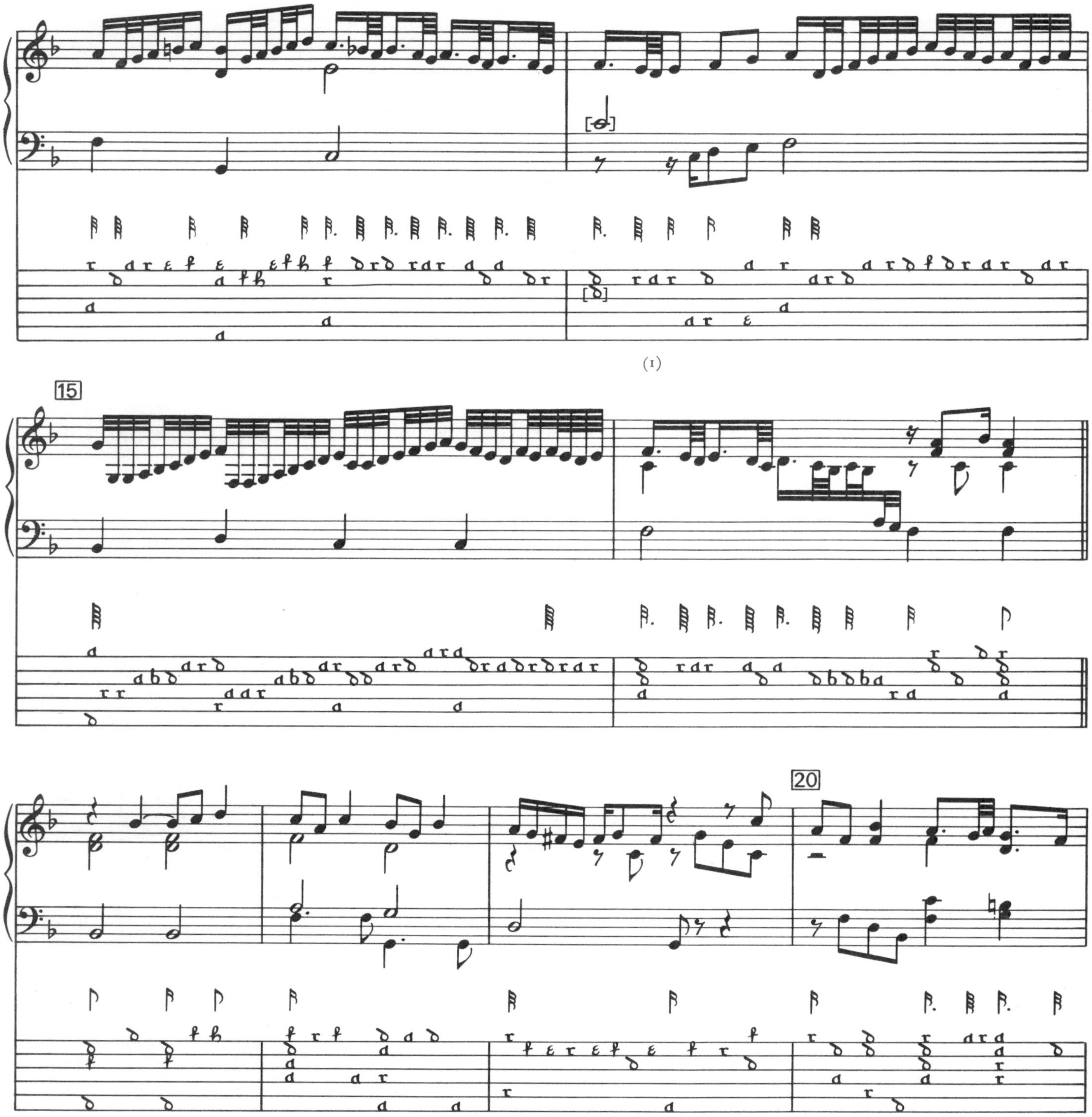

(1) d on 2 (2) r on 4 (3) d on 5.

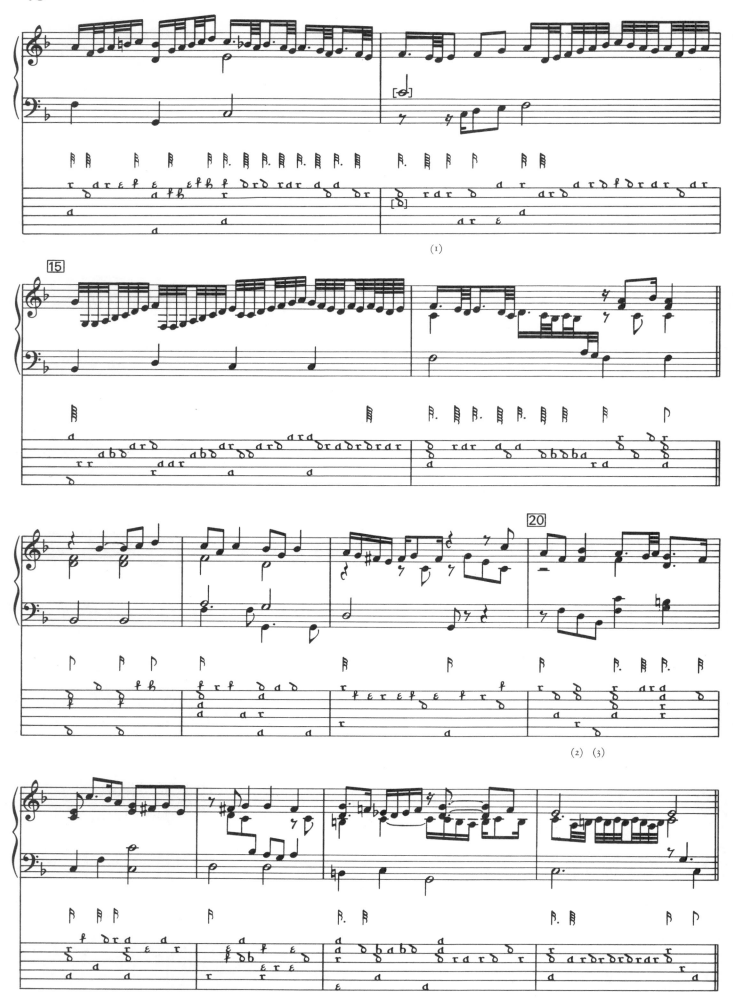

(4) ꞇ on 4 for ꞇ on 3 (5) This and the following three notes have been written one string higher. The correction has been made but without erasure of the higher notes. (6) An extra bar, filled with a decorative flourish, is added. See Notes.

11. Mrs. Brigide Fleetwood's Pavan
alias Solus Sine Sola

(1) **τ** on 2 (2) **d** on 4 added.

(3) **d** on 3, but cf. bar 7 (4) Notation confused. Reading from bar 27.

(5) **τ** one quaver earlier (6) **τ** on 2 added (7) Bar line omitted (8) **τ** on 5 (9) **ε** on 5 added (10) Time marks half correct value for one and a half bars (11) **d** on 6 under **h** on 2.

(12) ℰ on 1 added, then deleted (13) Bar lines absent (14) ♭ on 1 precedes ℰ on 4 (15) Bar line omitted.

12. Dr. Case's Pavan

(1) **d** on 6 (2) **d** on 2 added.

(3) ♭ on 3 (4) ♩ on 4.

13. Resolution

(1) d on 4.

(7) = ♪ (8) τ on 5 (9) = ♪ (10) ε on 7.

14. Mr. John Langton's Pavan

(1) ♮ on 3 written ♮ on 2 (2) = ♬ (3) ┌ on 4.

(4) Tablature confused. Next three notes from **TGG** and **Var.**

(5) τ on 6 (6) Corner of MS destroyed (7) ɑ on 3 (8) τ on 6 (9) ♭ on 1.

(10) **d** on 2 (11) Corner of MS destroyed.

14a. Sir John Langton's Pavan

(1) ε on 4 (2) = 𝅗𝅥 𝅘𝅥

(3) = 𝄽

(4) Tablature confused.

(5) Time marks confused till end of bar (6) 𝖽 on 1.

(7) = P (8) An extra four hemidemisemiquavers added.

15. Lachrimae

(1)

(2)

(3)

(4)

(1) ᴛ on 1 added (2) ♭ on 4 added (3) ᴛ on 4 and ᴛ on 5 added (4) ♭ on 3. For Galliard see p. 158.

(5) ♭ on 3 added (6) 𝄐 on 4 (7) ♮ on 2.

(8) ♭ on 2 added (9) τ on 4 for τ on 3.

(10) τ on 4 for τ on 3 (11) τ on 1 added.

16. A Pavan

(1) ♭ on 3 added (2) ♂ on 3.

(3) Tablature confused. Bar 26 substituted.

(4) **d** on 4.

(5) 4 extra beats added. See Notes.

17. The Lady Russell's Pavan

(1) **d** on 2 added (2) **τ** on 4.

(3) **d** on 1 added.

(4) Time values doubled till the half-bar (5) **d** on 6.

18. A Pavan

(1) **τ** on 4.

19. Captain Digorie Piper's Galliard

(1)

(2)

(1) See note **p. 318 (2)** ♭ on 6. For Pavan see p. 37.

(3) **d** on 4 (4) **ε** changed to **ð**.

(5) 𝄽 on 6 added.

20. Dowland's Galliard

(1) Bar line omitted (2) Last three bars from **Thy.**

21. John Dowland's Galliard

22. Dowland's First Galliard

(1) MS destroyed (2) See Notes (3) **r** on 5 scored through.

23. The Frog Galliard

(1) ꝺ on 3.

23a. The Frog Galliard

24. Galliard

(1) Bar taken from **30** (2) Rhythm from **30**.

25. Melancholy Galliard

(1) ♩ on 2 (2) ♩ on 2, ♩ on 3, ♪ on 4, ♯ on 5 (3) ♪ on 2 (4) ♩ on 2.

26. Sir John Souch's Galliard

(1) 𝆑 on 2 (2) 𝆏 on 3 and 𝆓 on 4.

27. A Galliard

(1) 𝆺 on 1 (2) 𝆺 on 3 (3) 𝅘 on 3.

28. A Galliard

(on a galliard by Daniel Bacheler)

29. Giles Hobie's Galliard

(1) ♮ on 1.

30. A Galliard

(1) ♩ on 2 (2) ♪ on 4 for ♪ on 3 (3) ♩ on 6.

(4) **b** on-3 added (5) **a** on 3.

31. A Galliard

(on Walsingham)

(1) ♮ on 6 (2) ♭ on 2 (3) ♩ on 3 (4) ♩ on 3 for ♩ on 4 (5) ♩ on 5 (6) ♭ on 3 (7) 𝄽 on 3.

32. Mrs. Vaux Galliard

(1) Tablature confused. Bar adopted from **TGG.** See Notes.

33. Mr. Langton's Galliard

(1) ♭ on 2 added.

(2) **d** on 6 added (3) **d** on 7, but cf. bar 57, and **G**.

34. Mignarda

(1) ʈ on 6 (2) ʈ on 5.

(3) **τ** on 4 (4) **τ** on 1 added (5) Bar missing (6) **ε** on 1 added (7) **♩** on 4 (8) **τ** on 1 added (9) **♩** on 1 (10) **♪** on 2.

35. A Galliard

36. Mr. Knight's Galliard

(1) on 7 (2) on 2.

37. My Lord Chamberlain, His Galliard

an invention for two to play upon one lute

(1) ⌐ placed over next note.

38. The Right Honourable
The Lord Viscount Lisle, His Galliard

(1) ♩ on 4.

(2) τ on ɪ.

(3) ♮ on 5 (4) Two notes wrongly marked 𝄽

39. Round Battle Galliard

(1) **b** on 3, **τ** on 4.

40. The Most High and Mighty Christianus the Fourth, King of Denmark, His Galliard

(1) ꝺ on 3.

(2) **d** on 7.

(3) **d** on 8.

41. *The Most Sacred Queen Elizabeth, Her Galliard*

42. Can She Excuse

42a. The Right Honourable Robert, Earl of Essex, His Galliard

43. *The Lady Rich's Galliard*

43a. The Right Honourable
The Lady Rich, Her Galliard

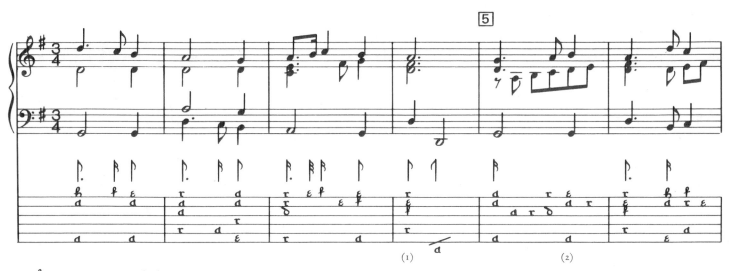

(1) ♯ on 4 (2) d on 6 on final quaver.

(3)

(4) **d** on 9.

44. The Earl of Derby's Galliard

(1) d on 6 (2) d on 6.

150

(3) Bar line absent (4) Bar line absent.

(5) ♩ on 1 added (6) Bar line absent (7) ♪. ♪ (incomplete bar) (8) ♩ on 1 added (9) Bar line.

44a. The Right Honourable Ferdinando, Earl of Derby, His Galliard

(1) **d** on 7.

45. The Right Honourable
The Lady Clifton's Spirit

(1) ♭ on 4.

(2) τ on 5 one semiquaver earlier (3) ᵈ on 4 one semiquaver earlier.

(4) τ on 1.

46. Galliard to Lachrimae

(1) **d** on 6, but cf. bar 4. For Pavan see p. 67.

47. *Sir John Smith, His Almain*

(1)

(2)

(3)

(1) ♭ on 2 for ♩ on 2 (2) = ♪♪   (3) ♮ on 1.

(4) ♭ (5) **d** on 5 (6) ♯ on 1.

47a. Smythes Allmayne

(1) d on 2.

48. Lady Laiton's Almain

48a. Lady Laiton's Almain

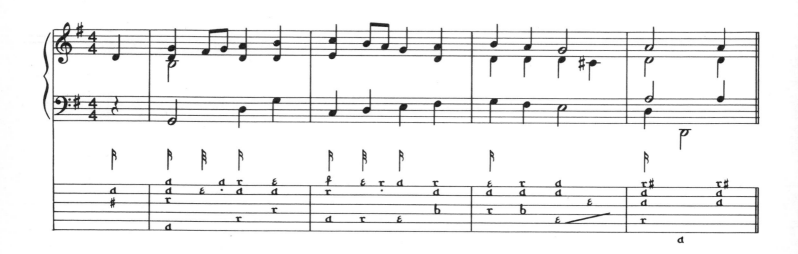

49. An Almain

(1) **d** on 3 placed under previous chord with ♭ time mark above. All following bar lines one beat later. The editors are grateful to Ian Harwood for suggesting this emendation. (2) First two signs in original ⊓ . The final strain is still only five bars long and it is possible that time values in the penultimate bar should be doubled.

50. Mrs. White's Thing

51. A Piece Without Title

(1) ε on 3 (2) Letter illegible (3) τ on 7 (4) d on 1.

52. Mrs. Nichols' Almain

53. Mrs. Clifton's Almain

(1) = ♭ (2) ♩ on 7.

54. Lady Hunsdon's Puffe

(1) Time marks in this bar from **FD.**

55. Mrs. Winter's Jump

56. Mrs. White's Nothing

57. Mrs Vaux's Jig

58. The Shoemaker's Wife.
A Toy

59. Tarleton's Riserrectione

60. Come Away

(Come Again)

61. Orlando Sleepeth

62. Fortune

(1) **d** on 5 in **Thy** and **WB** (2) Bar line omitted (3) **τ** on 6 in **WB** and **Myn.**

63. Complaint

64. Go From My Window

(1) Bar line missing.

(2) d on 1, but see Notes.

65. Lord Strang's March

66. My Lord Willoughby's
Welcome Home

66a. My Lord Willoughby's Welcome Home

(1) d on 1 for d on 2.

(2)   (3)

(2) 𝄐 on 4 for 𝄐 on 5 (3) 𝄐 on 6.

67. Walsingham

(1) ♭ on 2 for ♯ on 1 (2) ♮ on 4 for ♯ on 4 (3) ♮ on 3.

(4) ꝺ , ꝺ , ꞃ , ε one line higher.

(10) MS has double bar (11) **d** on 4 (12) **d** on 3.

(13) MS destroyed (14) MS destroyed (15) **d** on 1.

68. Aloe

(1)

(2) **d** on 2 (3) Bar line omitted.

(4) ♭ on 3 from **G**.

69. Loth to Depart

(1) MS destroyed (2) **d** on I.

(6) MS destroyed (7) 𝄿 on 6.

(8) ♮ on 3 (9) ♮ on 5 added (10) ♮ on 4.

70. Robin

(1) **τ** on 1 (2) **g** on 1.

(3) See Notes (4) ♭ on 2 added.

(5) **d** on 3 added.

71. A Fantasia

(1) Bars 20 and 21. Successive octaves as in source. Possibly **τ** on 1 for **ε** on 2? (2) **d** on 6.

(3) ꝺ ꝺ ꞇ written one line higher (4) ꝺ on 4.

72. A Fancy

(1) τ on 5.

(8) ε on 4 (9) ε on 3 added.

(10) ℰ on 4 (11) ♪ on 6.

73. A Fancy

(1)

(1) Bar line omitted.

(2) 𝅝 on 4 (3) Bar line omitted (4) 𝅗𝅥 on 6 (5) Bar line omitted (6) = 𝆏 (7) = 𝅘𝅥𝅮

(8) This note cannot, of course, be held for its full value on the lute (9) The preceding seven notes are repeated again before the bar line.

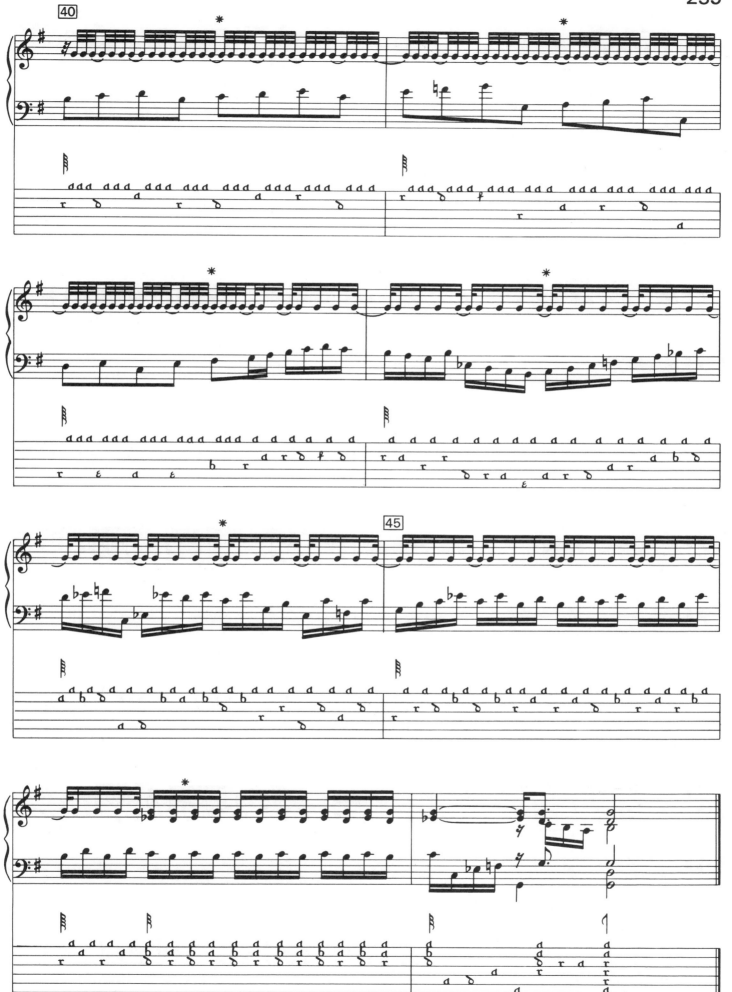

74. A Fancy

75. A Dream

(1) ꞇ present in **H** (2) ꝺ present in **H.**

(3) ε on 5 (4) d on 2, but ε in H.

76. A Galliard

(1) ♮ on 5 (2) ♭ on 4.

77. Mrs. Norrish's Delight

(1) ɛ on 5.

78. A Piece Without Title

(1)

(2)

(1) 𝄐 on 1, 𝄐 on 2, 𝄐 on 3 (2) Time marks and bar lines confused at this point.

79. *What If A Day*

(1) From here to the end the value of the time marks is halved in the MS.

80. A Coy Joy

(1) An extra note (♮?) added.

81. Tarleton's Jig

82. A Galliard

(1) ♭ on 2 added (2) ♭ on 1 (3) ♭ on 3.

83. Dowland's Galliard

84. Hasellwood's Galliard

85. Galliarda Dulandi 39

86. Pauana Dulandi

(1) ♭ on 2 for ♭ on 3.

87. Galliarda Dulandi 8

(1) ♭ on 2 (2) ♮ on 3.

88. Piper's Galliard

(1) ♮ on 6 and ♦ on 7 (2) ♮ on 6.

(3) Bar line omitted.

(4) τ on 4 (5) Time marks confused (6) Bar line placed after **d** on 6 (7) Bar line omitted.

89. Can She Excuse

(1) **d** on 7 (2) ⊃ on 1.

(3) = ♪. ♪ (4) **ɑ** on 4 placed between ♯ and ♭ on 1.

90. The Frog Galliard

(1) ♭ on 3.

(2) Covered by ink blots (3) MS obscure.

91. Suzanna Galliard

92. Galliard Fr. Cutting

(1) τ on 1.

93. Del Excellentissimo Musico
Jano Dulando
(Une Jeune Fillette)

(2) ♭ on 3 added in original (3) τ on 2 (4) ε on 5.

274

(5) ♭ on 5 (6) ε on 3 (7) ε on 3.

(8)

(8) ♭ on 3.

(9) ♭ on 3 followed by ♮ on 3.

(10) ♭ on 3 (11) This and the following note written in reverse order.

(15) Don 1.

(16) **d** under **g** on 2 preceding.

94. Pavana Johan Douland

(1) ♮ in original (2) ♮. ♮ in original.

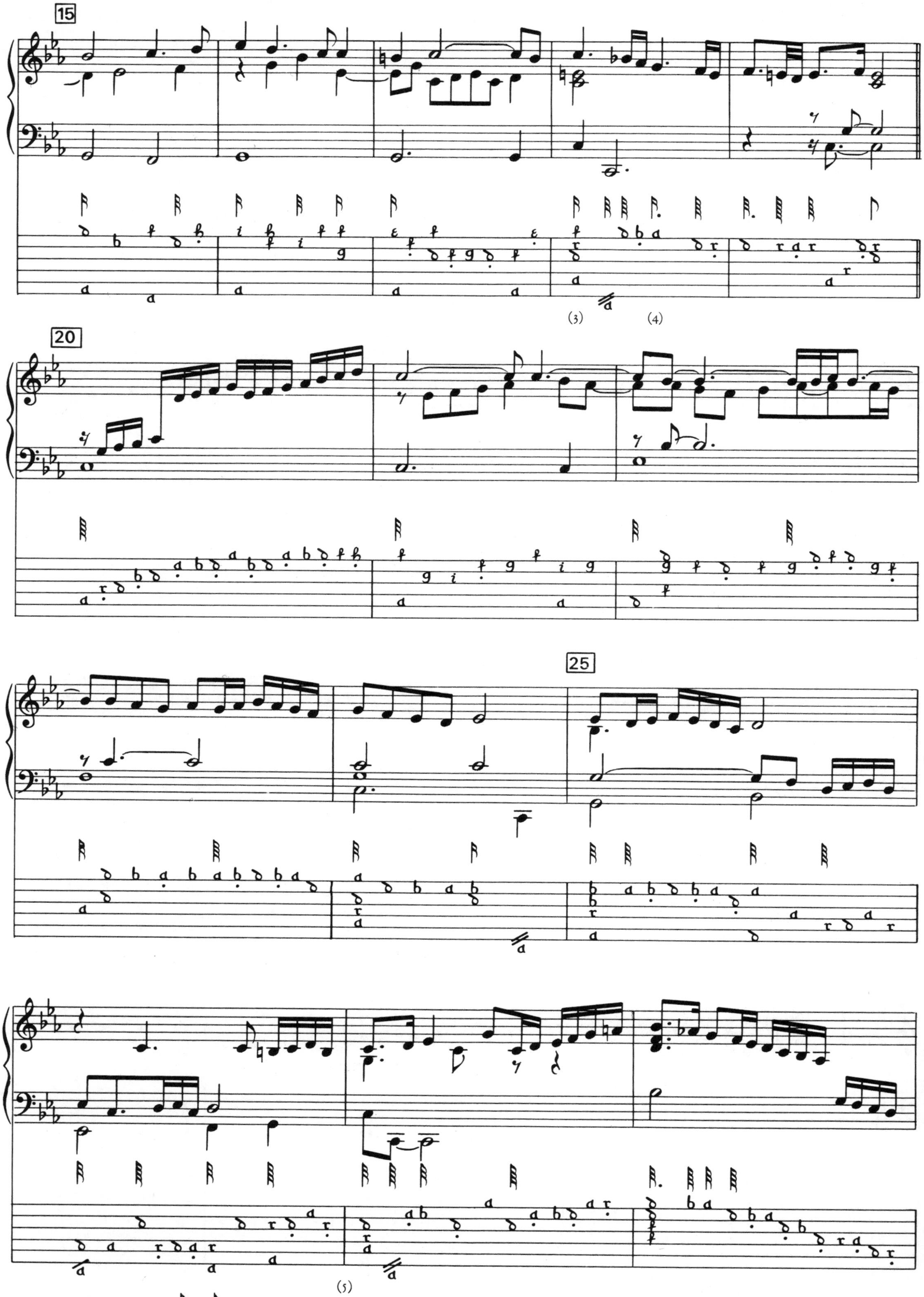

(3) r on 4 for a on 5 (4) in original (5) Bar line 1 beat earlier.

(6) **d** on 7 but cf. bar 11 (7) **d** on 1 (8) ♫ in original.

(9) 𝄽 in original (10) 𝅗 on 7 but cf. bar 70.

(11) ♭ on 4 (12) ♩ on 4 (13) ♩ on 8 but cf. bar 50 (14) ♭ on 2 added in original but cf. bar 53.

(15) d on 4 but cf. bar 109 (16) d on 8 and b on 4, followed by b on 4 (17) d on 8.

(18) ♯ on 1, but cf. bar 85 (19) Time mark omitted (20) Bar line 1 beat earlier (21) 𝑔 on 3. Time mark ♩ (22) 𝑖 on 2 (23) 𝄾 on 4.

95. La Mia Barbara

(6) τ on 3 added, but cf. bar 54 (7) Dot omitted.

(8)

(8) **d** on 8, but cf. bar 41.

(12) ε on 4 in original, but cf. bar 91 (13) Time mark omitted (14) 2 bars omitted. 67 and 68 inserted.

(15) Time mark omitted (16) 𝖽 on 7 (17) ♮ on 5 instead of ♯ on 4, but cf. bar 74.

96. An Almand

(1) = ♪ ♫   𝄽 on 7 (3) 𝄽 on 7 (4) 𝄽 on 7.

(5) = 𝅗𝅥, but cf. bar 20.

97. The Queen's Galliard

(2) Sic. Also in **D2**.

98. Preludium

99. *Mr. Dowland's Midnight*

100. Coranto

101. Phantasia

102. Praeambulum

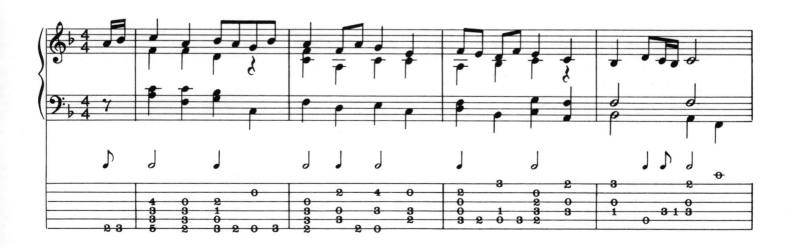

103. Gagliarda

104. Galliard

(1)

(2)

(1) ⊓ placed over these notes (2) Bar line placed one beat earlier.

(3) These two letters are placed as τ on 2 for δ on 2, and δ on 5 for τ on 5.

(4) ♭ on 3 added.

105. *Galliarda Douland Cantus*

(1)

(1) Time marks in this bar in original =

List of sources, abbreviations used and the pieces in this collection contained in each

ENGLISH

Printed Books

Bk. 1 John Dowland, *The First Booke of Songes* (1597, 1600, 1603, 1606, probably 1608, and 1613)
37. (see also 19, 23a, 24, 26)

Bk. 2 John Dowland, *The Second Booke of Songes* (1600)
13. (see also 15)

LoST John Dowland, *Lachrimae or Seaven Teares* (1604). For five viols or violins and lute. This is not a source for solo music, but it frequently casts valuable light on those pieces that exist both in solo and in consort form.

MB Robert Dowland, *A Musicall Banquet* (1610)
38.

NCL Thomas Robinson, *New Citharen Lessons* (1609)
42.

PS John Dowland, *A Pilgrimes Solace* (1612)
46. (see also 34)

Var Robert Dowland, *Varietie of Lute-Lessons* (1610)
1a, 14a, 40, 41, 42a, 43a, 44a, 45, 47.

WB William Barley, *A New Booke of Tabliture* (1596)
8, 10, 15, 42, 55, 62, 64.

Manuscripts

CAMBRIDGE UNIVERSITY LIBRARY

27 Add.2764 (2) (fragmentary)
15, 21, 47, 48, 50, 85.

30 Add.3056
1, 5, 6, 8, 15, 17, 19, 23a, 24, 42, 88, 89, 90.

CCB Dd.4.23
19, 22, 41, 48, 50, 63.

D2 Dd.2.11.(B)
8, 10, 12, 15, 19, 20, 21, 22, 23, 24, 25, 31, 34, 41, 42, 45, 48, 49, 50, 52, 56, 61, 63, 65, 66, 75, 81, 85, 91, 97.

D4 Dd.4.22
62.

D5 Dd.5.78.(3) (E)
3, 14, 15, 16, 17, 18, 19, 26, 27, 28, 29, 30, 31, 34, 36, 43, 44, 51, 54, 58, 64, 68, 92.

D9 Dd.9.33.(C)
2, 4, 6, 7, 11, 17, 18, 19, 32, 33, 34, 35, 36, 40, 43, 53, 54, 57, 58, 67, 69, 70, 73, 76, 82, 84, 88.

N6 Nn.6.36.(B)
6, 13, 42, 44, 60, 83.

BRITISH MUSEUM

31 Add.31392
1, 8, 10, 15, 19, 55, 74, 85.

38 Add.38539
1, 15, 28, 40, 47a, 50, 83.

64 Add.6402
15, 54.

H Hirsch MS 1353
15, 19, 21, 42, 75, 84, 104.

JP Eg.2046
1, 8, 9, 15, 40, 43, 50, 64, 66, 70, 71.

GLASGOW UNIVERSITY LIBRARY

G R.d.43 The Euing Lute Book
1, 3, 7, 8, 9, 10, 15, 17, 19, 22, 23, 25, 28, 33, 42, 44, 52, 53, 55, 62, 64, 66, 68, 72, 76, 78, 85.

FITZWILLIAM MUSEUM, Cambridge

LHC Lord Herbert of Cherbury's Lute Book
15, 28, 29 ("Gagliarda J: Doulande", f. 54v=lute part of "Giles Hoby's Galliard" in **LoST**).

TRINITY COLLEGE, Dublin

BD D.1.21 Ballet's Lute Book
47, 61, 62.

ARCHBISHOP MARSH'S LIBRARY, Dublin

Mar Z.3.2.13
43, 47, 77, 85.

In the possession of LORD FORESTER

W The Weld Lute Book
9, 15, 40, 43, 44, 48, 62, 83.

In the possession of the MARQUESS OF DOWNSHIRE. Deposited in the Berkshire County Record office, Reading.

Tru Trumbull Add. MS 6
68.

In the possession of MR. ROBERT SPENCER

Bro The Browne Bandora and Lyra Viol Book
69.

Board The Margaret Board Lute Book
10, 15, 19, 22, 28, 40, 61.

Myn The Mynshall Lute Book
21, 43, 48, 61, 62, 66, 80, 83.

Tol The Tollemache Lute Book
40, 44, 50, 66a.

YALE UNIVERSITY LIBRARY

Wi The Wickhambrook Lute Book
48, 50, 59, 66.

THE FOLGER LIBRARY, Washington

FD MS 1610.1 The Dowland Lute Book
15, 23a, 39, 40, 42, 47, 48a, 53, 54, 55, 66a, 79, 83.

FOREIGN'

Printed Books

BNP J-B. Besardus, *Novus Partus* (Augsburg, 1617)
15, arranged for three lutes.

BTH J-B. Besardus, *Thesaurus Harmonicus* (Cologne, 1603)
1, 15, 19, 48a, and D. Bacheler's Galliard, **38**, f. 15, wrongly ascribed to Dowland.

DM Joachim van den Hove, *Delitæ Musica* (Utrecht, 1612)
8, 48 and seven lute parts from **LoST**.

Flo   Joachim van den Hove, *Florida* (Utrecht, 1601)
15, 42, 61.

FM   Johannes Rude, *Flores Musicæ* (Heidelberg, 1598)
11, 15, 52.

MHM   Elias Mertel, *Hortus Musicalis Novus* (Strasbourg, 1615)
2, 6.

NGC   Adrianus Valerius, *Nederlandtsche Gedenck-Clanck* (Haarlem, 1626)
15, 23a.

SdM   Nicolas Vallet, *Le Secret des Muses* (Amsterdam, 1618)
42 (not by Dowland), 66.

TGG   Georg Leopold Fuhrmann, *Testudo Gallo-Germanica* (Nürnberg, 1615)
3, 14, 15, 28, 32, 40, 42, 48, 61, 70.

Manuscripts

B   Berlin, Preussiche Staatsbibliothek Mus. MS. 40141
15, 42, 47, 52.

Brahe   Per Brahes Visbok, Skoklosters Castle Library, Sweden
1, 23, 40, 43, 47.

Dol   Haslemere, Surrey, the Dolmetsch Library, B.II.1
15, 19.

Eys   Elizabeth Eysbock's Keyboard Book, Royal Swedish Academy of Music, Stockholm, Sweden. Tablature No. 1.
8, 15, 42, 52.

Fab   København, Det Kongelige Bibliotek, Thott, 841.40 Fabritius MS
15, 50.

Hain   The Hainhofer MS, Wolfenbüttel
42.

K10   Kassel, Landesbibliothek, 4° Mus. 108.1
8, 15, 28, 42, 60, 61.

L   Leipzig, Stadtbibliothek, II.6.15
10, 15, 23, 43, 48, 49, 52, 55, 60, 85, 86, 87.

Linz   Linzer Lautenbuch, Vienna, Oberösterreichischen Landesarchiv, Nr. 18, 1977.
8, 15, 23, 42, 48, 62.

Lvov   Lvov Scientific Library, Academy of the Ukraine, USSR.
Lute Tablature MS No. 1400.
2, 3, 6.

Mylius   Johannes Mylius, *Thesaurus* (Frankfurt, 1622)
3, 6.

NS   Prague, University Library. 485 XXII. F.174 (1608) Nicolao Schmall's MS
61.

Nür   Nürnberg, Germ. Nat. Mus. Hs. 33648, 1
23, 23a, 42, 43, 105.

Sch   The Schele Lute MS, Hamburg Staats- und Universitätsbibliothek MB/2768 (Formerly Real. ND. VI, No. 3238).
23, 43, 44, 47a, 48a, 93, 94, 95.

Slo   London, British Museum. Sloane 1021
15.

Thy   Leiden, Bibl. Thysiana, Thysius MS
15, 20, 23, 35, 42, 43, 47, 48, 61, 62, 85.

MS known to have contained works by Dowland, now destroyed
Dresden, Sachs. Landesbibliothek. Mus. MS 1.V.8
Loss MS

MSS containing works by Dowland, whereabouts now unknown
Robert Gordon of Straloch's Lute Book
MS formerly in the possession of Lord Braye.
Reports of the Historical Manuscript Commission, Vol. 15. (1885–1887) p. 108

Miscellaneous abbreviations

BM   British Museum, London

CNRS   Centre Nationale de la Recherche Scientifique, Paris

FVB   Fitzwilliam Virginals Book, edited by J. A. Fuller Maitland and W. Barclay Squire (1899) from the MS in the Fitzwilliam Museum, Cambridge

WT   Without title

EDITORIAL NOTES

The various versions of the pieces listed in these notes are, with the exception of Dowland's re-use of his own material in the song books and in **LoST,** confined to those written for the lute, and, unless otherwise stated, are presumed to be by Dowland himself. Various composers made use of Dowland's material and arranged his pieces for cittern, virginals, consorts, etc., and ballad writers adopted some of his tunes; none of these is mentioned unless a point of special interest is involved.

Unless a diapason is indicated, a six-course lute is understood. If the arrangement of the strains and their repeats differs in other sources from the lay-out of the chosen version, the variant will be shown: A representing the first strain, A' its repeat; B the second strain, B' its repeat, etc.
For more detailed information about many of the pieces, origins of some of the melodies, notes on arrangements for other instruments, and discussion of the meaning of certain of the titles, see Diana Poulton *John Dowland* (Faber and Faber, 1972).

Where there is more than one source the first is that given in the text.

1. **31** ff. 13v 14/14v "A fantasie Maister Dowland" Diapason at D.
   30 ff. 8v/9 WT "John Dowlande BM" Diapason at D.
   G ff. 16v/17 WT Anon. Diapason at D.
   JP ff. 24v/25 "A Fantasia" Anon. Diapason at D.
   38 ff. 14v/15 WT Anon. Heavily ornamented and marked with fingering points and hold signs. Eight courses indicated.
   BTH ff. 170v/171/171v "Fantasia Ioannis Doolandi". Contains many errors and should not be used as a source.

All versions except **38** are for a seven-course lute with the diapason at D. The opening theme is one used by other composers of the time and may have been based on the first few bars of an Italian *lauda*.

Bar	beat	source	variant
Bar 5	beat 3	JP G	c on 2 added
	3 & 4	38	[music notation]
6	1	JP 30	a on 2 added
	3	JP 30 38	c on 2 added
	4	G	[music notation]
7	1	30	a on 7 instead of c on 5
	1 & 2	JP	[music notation]
		38	[music notation]
Bar 7	beat 2	G 30	[music notation]
	3	G	c on 4 omitted
	4	G	a on 3 omitted
8	1 & 2	JP 30 38	[music notation]
	2	G	[music notation], but c on 4 omitted
	3	G JP	e on 5 omitted
	3	G	[music notation]
9	1	G JP	c on 5 omitted
	2	G	c on 4 omitted
	3	G 30 38	[music notation]
10	1	JP	a on 7 instead of c on 5
13	4	38	a on 6
14	3	G	[music notation], h on 3 on the ½ beat omitted
	4	30 JP 38	[music notation]
16	1	G	d on 3 and c on 4 omitted c on 2 added
	2	G JP	a on 3 omitted
	3	G 38	c on 4 omitted
		38	a on 2 added
Bar 16	beat 3	JP	e on 1, a on 2 and a on 6
	4	G	c on 1 omitted
After bar 17		30	[music notation]
18	4	JP	c on 4 omitted
		G	c on 3 instead of c on 4
23	1 2nd q.	JP	f on 3 instead of e on 2
	3	JP 30 38	[music notation]
		JP G	a on 7 instead of h on 6
		G	f on 2 instead of a on 3
24	1	JP 38	a on 2
	2 1st sq.	JP	e on 2
	3 & 4	30	[music notation]
	4	JP 38	[music notation]
25	1	30	c on 1, a on 2, a on 3, c on 5
		38	c on 1, a on 2,

Bar	beat	source	reading
Bar 25 beat	1	**38**	a on 3, a on 8
	2 1st sq.	**G**	a on 5 omitted
26	2	**30 G**	b on 4 instead of e on 7
	3	**30 G**	e on 5 instead of c on 7
27	1	**30**	c on 5 instead of a on 7
		G	a on 2 and c on 5 only
		JP	e on 2, a on 3, c on 5 and a on 7
27	3	**30**	c on 5 omitted
28	1	**G 30**	c on 5 instead of a on 7
	1 2nd sq.	**JP**	e on 4 omitted
29		**30**	MS confused
35	1 2nd sq	**30**	a on 1

(musical notation)

	3	**JP**	(musical notation)
36	1	**JP**	c on 3 added
	4	**JP**	a on 3 omitted
37	1	**38**	a on 2 added
After bar 39		**30**	(musical notation)

(musical notation)

40		**30**	(musical notation)
41	1 1st q.	**G**	e on 6
	1 2nd q.	**G**	a on 1 and c on 3

(musical notation)

43	1 & 2	**JP**	(musical notation)
44	4	**30**	g on 4 omitted

(musical notation)

45	2 & 3	**JP**	(musical notation)
46	1	**G JP 30 38**	c on 5 added
		JP	a on 3 omitted
	3 2nd q.	**G 30**	a on 6 omitted
47	1	**JP**	a on 2 and c on 4 added
		30	e on 1, a on 2 c on 4
		38	e on 1, a on 2, c on 4, a on 6
50	1 2nd q.	**JP**	c on 4 omitted
	3	**38**	e on 1 and a on 2 only
	4	**JP 38**	c on 4 added
	4 2nd q.	**G**	e on 4 added
51	last note	**JP**	e on 2

(musical notation)

| 52 | | **30** | (musical notation) |

Bar	beat	source	reading
Bar 52 beat	3	**38 JP**	c on 5 omitted
	3 2nd note	**JP**	a on 7
53	3 2nd q.	**JP**	a on 1, a on 2, c on 4 omitted
55	3 2nd q.	**38**	c on 5 instead of c on 4
56	1	**38 JP**	a on 6 instead of c on 4
	4	**30**	f on 6 added
		JP	c on 6; a on 1 omitted
		G	a on 5 added
	2nd q.	**JP**	c on 6 omitted
57	2	**JP**	a on 7 instead of c on 5
59	2	**JP**	a on 7 instead of c on 5
61	2	**JP**	a on 7 instead of c on 5
63	2	**JP**	a on 7 instead of c on 5
68	4	**JP**	a on 1
72	4	**JP G**	a on 5 under 1st sq.
73	1 4th sq.	**JP**	d on 3
74		**G**	a 2/4 bar bringing the bar line forward 2 beats
		38	shake prolonged till end of bar; last 4 beats of 74 become 1st 4 of 75
75	1	**JP**	a on 6 added
76	2	**JP**	a on 7 instead of c on 5
78	2	**JP 30 G**	e on 1 omitted
78	last note	**JP**	dot omitted; e on 1 = (note) on 1st beat of 79
79	3 2nd note	**JP**	a on 7 instead of c on 5
81	10th q.	**38**	a on 2 added
82		**JP**	last 3 qs. omitted and bar line brought forward, till 93
84	4th q.	**38**	c on 3 omitted
	7th q.	**38**	a on 6 instead of c on 4
86	8th q.	**JP**	e on 6
88	1st q.	**G**	e of next bar brought forward
90	1	**30**	c on 1 omitted

(musical notation)

	1st, 2nd, 3rd qs. **JP**		(musical notation)
91	1	**30**	a on 1 omitted
91	1 2nd q.	**G**	a on 6
92	last 6 qs.	**G**	omitted
93		**JP**	begins after 3rd q. of 92:

3rd q. **38** a on 1 added

1a. **Var** Fantasie No. 7. "Composed by John Douland, Bachelar of Musicke". Diapason at D.

This version appears to have been revised by Dowland himself for inclusion in **Var**. The fact that the earlier version is found in later MSS such as **38** and **JP** suggests the piece continued to be played in its original form after the publication of **Var** in 1610.

2. **D9** ff. 16v/17. "forlorne Hope fancye Mr Dowland Bach of Musicke". Diapason at D.

MHM No. 70, pp. 210/211. WT Anon. Bars half the length of those in D9. Diapasons at F and D.

Bar 5 beat 1 **MHM** e on 2, b on 3, c on 5

8	4	
15	1	c on 4 instead of on 3
16	4	c on 6 omitted
18	4	= ; c on 2, d on 3, the following a on 2 omitted
20	4	e on 4 omitted
24	4	c on 6 omitted
26	2	d on 2
	4	f on 2 instead of b on 3
27	1	
33		the notes of the descending chromatic hexachord are given correctly

3. **D5** ff. 43v/44. "farwell Jo: dowlande". The title and name are in Dowland's own hand. Diapason at D.

G ff. 41v/42. WT Anon. Diapason at D.

Bar	beat		
29	1	**G**	a on 6 omitted
36	4	**G**	c on 4 omitted
41	4	**G**	f on 2 omitted
43	1	**G**	c on 4 omitted
44	2	**G**	e on 4 omitted

4. **D9** ff. 41v/42. "Farwell Jo. Dowlande". Diapason at D.

D9 f. 50v. WT Anon. Another copy, as far as bar 35 only. The MS of this In Nomine is extremely confused and the solution of its many problems is due to the work of Mr. Richard Newton. Particularly in the writing of the time marks the scribe has left many ambiguous passages.

5. **30** ff. 17v/18. WT. "J. Dowland". Diapason at D.

6. **30** ff. 7v/8. "A Fancy by Mr. Dowlande BM" Diapason at D.

D9 ff. 43v/44. WT. Anon. Diapason at D.

N6 ff. 32v/33. WT. Anon. Diapason at D.

MHM No. 69. pp. 208/209/210. WT. Anon. Diapason at D.

All copies have minor variants as well as errors and omissions. **MHM** has half-length bars which are regular throughout. MS copies are all barred differently and irregularly.

Bar 10 beat 3 to bar 12 beat 2 **MHM** Time values halved

11	3 to	12	2	Dotted rhythm omitted
16	1 & 2			=
22	3 to	25	2	Time values halved
28 & 29	4			Dotted rhythm omitted
34	3 & 4			Omitted
38	3	2nd note in bass		c on 4
	4	**N6**		Last 2 notes transposed
		MHM D9		b on 3
39	last 2 notes			
		MHM D9		Position transposed

46 beat 2	**N6**	

7. **D9** ff. 6v/7/7v. "A fancy Jo Dow". Diapason at D.

G ff. 35/35v/36. WT. Anon. Diapason at D.

G has a number of errors and is a less reliable text. There are however, a few genuine variants:

Bar 20 & 21 beat 4 4 last notes only, with

42	4	d on 1 added

56	2	

8. **D2** ff. 46v/47. "Pauen J.D.". AA'BB'C.

JP ff. 19v/20. "Pipers Pavinge my Mr dowlande". AA'BB'CC'.

30 ff. 2v/3. "Pipers Pauan by John Dowlande BM". AA'BB'CC'.

31 ff. 27v/28. "Mayster Pypers Pavyn by Mayster Dowland". AA'BB'C.

G f. 29v. WT. Anon. A B C only.

WB No. 4. "Pipers Pauin By I.D.". AA'BB'CC'.

DM f. 37v. "Pavana Pijper", "Dovvlant". A B C only.

K10 f. 70v/71. "pipers paduan". Anon. A B C.

D2, JP and **31** agree fairly closely, although **JP** and **31** have half-length bars. **30,** as usual, is individual in its treatment. **WB** is generally unsatisfactory; so too, are the foreign versions. The original composition may have had no division to the last strain. The one given by **JP** is exceedingly simple and that of **30** is almost certainly composed by the compiler of the MS. This division from **30** has, however, been included in the transcription since it shows how such a passage would have been treated by an independent and competent musician.

Bars 8 & 9 **30** Compressed into one bar

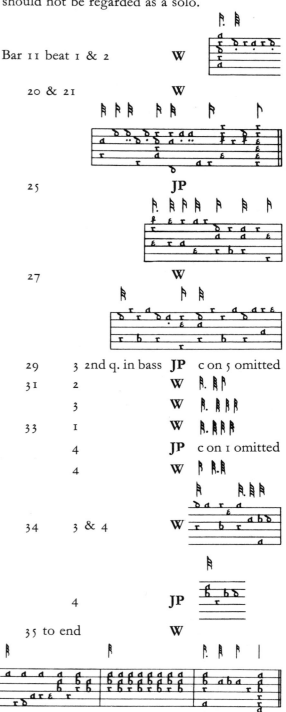

Bar 16   30

17 beats 3 & 4   **WB**

31

30

Time marks confused on last four notes

21   30

38-42   30

43-50   **JP**

9. **G** f. 25. WT. Anon. Diapason at D.
  W f. 14v. "Semper dolens". Anon. Diapason at D.
  JP f. 31v. "Dowlandes Lamentation 'Semp dolent' ". Adapted for a six-course lute by omitting all notes that fall on the 7th, with disastrous effects on the harmony.
  LoST No. 8. "Semper Dowland semper dolens".

DM ff. 38v/39. "Semper Dowlant semper dolens", "Ioan Doulant". Reprint of the lute part from **LoST**.
There can be no doubt that the MSS give an earlier version of the piece than that of **LoST**, which has been modified in some passages to adapt it to the consort form. This lute part should not be regarded as a solo.

Bar 11 beat 1 & 2   **W**

20 & 21   **W**

25   **JP**

27   **W**

29   3 2nd q. in bass   **JP**   c on 5 omitted
31   2   **W**
     3   **W**
33   1   **W**
     4   **JP**   c on 1 omitted
     4   **W**

34   3 & 4   **W**

4   **JP**

35 to end   **W**

10. **G** ff. 27v/28. WT. Anon. Diapason at D.
  D2 f. 58v. "Solus cũ sola J Dowl".
  31 ff. 14v/15. "Solus cũ sola Dowland".
  WB No. 11. "Solus cum sola made by I.D." (Orpharion) A B C only. Diapason at F.
The last two versions have half-length bars.
WB is very erratic in the use of time marks.
For a discussion of the meaning of the titles of this pavan and No. 11, see Diana Poulton *John Dowland* (Faber and Faber, 1972) p. 120.
Possibly the refrain of the old counting song "The Dilly Song", *Faber Book of Popular Verse*, edited Geoffrey Grigson, 1971, p. 28, "One is

one and all alone / And ever more shall be so",
is a reference to the same ideas.

    Bars 9–16 **D2** This division has numerous
           differences from the other two
           sources.

Bar 40 beats 3 & 4   **31**

40 (extra beats)   **G**

11. **D9** ff. 33v/34. "Mrs Brigide fleetwoods pauen
    als Solus sine sola Jo Dowland".
    FM Liber Secundus No. 110. "Paduana I.D"

Bar 18 original **D9**
      reading

12. **D2** f. 14v. "Dr Cases Pauen J. Dowland".
    In the song "Farewell, unkind, farewell", **Bk. 3**,
    No. XIV, Dowland re-uses the material of the
    last five bars of this pavan.
13. **N6** ff. 18/18v. "resoluc͡on". Anon. Diapason
    at D.
    Bk. 2. "Dowlands Adew for Master Oliver
    Cromwell". For lute and bass viol. Diapason
    at D.
14. **D5** ff. 2v/3. WT. Anon. Diapason at D.
    TGG p. 53. "Pavana Englesa Tertia". Anon.
    Diapason at D.
    This version, though printed after the appear-
    ance of **Var**, reproduces the earlier form. It has
    a number of errors. Hardly any passages could
    be regarded as genuine variants.
    LoST No. 10. "M. John Langtons Pavan"
    (in F). A B C.
14a.**Var** Pavan No. 5. "Sir John Langton his
    Pauin". Diapasons at F and D.

There are two distinct versions of this piece.
D5, TGG, LoST have much in common,
especially in strain B, which, in these three cases,
has 7 bars, while in **Var** it has 8. In addition
in **Var** an extra beat has been created in strain
B, bar 2, which changes the position of the bar
lines and the strong beats of the earlier version
become the weak beats of the later. The title
"Mr John Langton's Pavan" has been adopted
for the earlier form of the solo, since it was,
presumably, written before Langton received
his knighthood in 1603.
    14 and 14a. Bar 18, beat 1 2nd sq. The reading
of **LoST** would give this G as sharp.

15. **D5** ff. 9v/21. WT. "J:D".
    D2 f. 81. WT. Anon. Originally written for
    a 6 course lute, but in a few places a on 7
    has been added. So, too, have a few orna-
    ment signs.
    These two copies probably represent the
    original form of the piece. They differ notably
    from most later versions by omitting the dotted
    rhythm of bars 27, 28, 29 and 30.
    JP ff. 16v/17. "Lacrime by Dowland". Though
    late, this copy shares most of the charac-
    teristics of the early version, including the
    absence of the dotted rhythm.
    31 ff. 35v/36. "Dowlands Lachrimæ maister
    Dowland". A good version, but contains
    many scribal errors.
    G ff. 25v/26. WT. Anon. Diapason at D, but
    the two occasions on which it is used are
    quite arbitrary and the upper octave c on 5
    has not been removed.
    38 ff. 22v/23. "Lacrime Pauin by Mr John
    Dowland". Diapason at D. Where the
    diapason is used the higher octave is omitted.
    Heavily ornamented and marked with finger-
    ing points.
    W f. 4v. "Pauana Lachrimæ by Mr. Dowland".
    Occasional ornament signs and fingering
    points.
    LHC f. 8v. "Pauana by J. Dowlande Lach-
    rimæ". Diapason at D, used frequently on
    the dominant chord.
    FD ff. 18v/19. "Lacrame mr Dowland". A
    text with many variants from the norm.
    WB No. 3. "Lacrime by I.D.". Another
    unusual text.
    64 f. 1. "Lacrame". Anon. A B C only.
    H f. 11v. WT. Anon. In A mi. A B C only.
    Not the lute part of **LoST**.
    D2 ff. 75v/77. "Lachrimæ Jo: Dowl". In A mi.
    Diapason at D. Departs in many details
    from the more generally accepted version
    and is probably an arrangement.
    30 ff. 4v/5. "Lachrimæ by MR Dowlande, BM".
    30 ff. 14v/15. WT. Anon.
    30 ff. 36v/37. "Lacrimæ CK".
    These three last arrangements depart from the
    norm in many passages. They are almost
    certainly not by Dowland.
    27 ff. [5v]/[6]. "Dowlandes Lacrimæ". In
    A mi. A B C only.
    Bk. 2 No. 2. "Flow my teares". The second of
    the "Songs to two voices".

Some foreign versions

Printed books
    BTH ff. 16v/17. "Fantasia Ioannis Dowland
    Angli Lachrimæ". Diapason at D.
    BNP No. 7. "Lachrimæ J. Dooland a I.B.B. in

hanc concert. accommodatæ" for three lutes, with parts for Superius and Bassus.

Flo ff. 94/94v/95. "Pavana Lachrime" and "Reprinse".

FM Liber Secundus, No. 91. "Pavana a 5 voc. Dulandi Angli".

TGG p. 60. "Pavana Lachrimae V.S." (Valentinius Strobelius).

NGC p. 116. "Pavane Lachrimæ met den Bass". Anon.

MSS

K10 ff. 5/5v. "pavana lacrima". Anon.
ff. 55v/56. "pavana lacrima". Anon.

L p. 79. "Pavana Lachrijmæ". Anon. (German tab.).

B ff. 36v/37/37v/38. "Fantasia Joannis Dulandi".

Thy f. 388v. "Lacrime". Anon.
f. 389v. "Lacryme". Anon. For second lute or consort?

Fab f. 109v. "Lacrime Angelica" (German tab.).

Slo f. 21v. "Pavan Lacrymae". Anon.

Dol ff. 225v-227v. "Lachrymæ". Anon. (French tab.). G mi. Six courses.

Of all Dowland's compositions "Lachrimæ" was the most widely known. It was appreciated at a popular level as well as by those with cultivated musical taste. Not only were arrangements made for many different instruments but a number of composers adopted the opening phrase as a basis for their own compositions. Several of the settings in the English lute MSS have divisions to the repeats that are quite unlike Dowland's own very personal style and are almost certainly the work of his contemporaries.

The piece was well-known on the continent and it is found in a number of books and MSS, but in general the versions are poor and though they are listed here they are not treated in detail. No account has been given of the versions for bandora, virginals, lyra viol, recorder, cittern or consort; the lute solo in its various forms only having a place here. The lute part in **LoST** has a number of features which are not present in the solo version. In particular it should be noted that the suspended seventh from bar 1, beat 4, to bar 2, beat 1, belongs purely to the version with viols and is not found in the true solo "Lachrimæ". Originally written for a six-course lute, in the key of G minor, it is quite complete in this form although in later copies the diapason D is often added to the dominant chord. Even of the most generally accepted form no two copies are identical, each having its own omissions, additions and small alterations.

Bar	beat			
2	1	**LHC** 31 38		♩ ♪♪
	2	1	**W**	c on 4 added
	4	3	**W** 38	♪ ♪
	5	1	**W D2 JP** 38	♩ ♪
	7	3	**W**	e on 4 added
	9	3 & 4 38		*(notation)*

Bar	beat			
10	1	**JP**	a on 1 added
	1 last sq.	**JP** 38	e on 2
11	2 nd sq.	**JP**	d on 3
12	last chord	**D2 JP LHC**	c on 1 omitted
		W 38 31	c on 1 present
13	1	31 38 **W**	♩ ♪ ♪
	2 3rd sq.	**W**	c on 4 omitted
15	3	**W**	e on 4 omitted
19	1	**JP**	a on 2, b on 3 added. These notes omitted from next chord
	2	38	*(notation)*
	3 2nd q.	**W**	d on 3 added
	4	**LHC** 31 38 **W**	♩ ♪ ♪
26	4	**LHC** 31 38 **W**	♪ ♩ ♩
27	1 & 2	38 **W**	♩ ♪ ♩ ♪♪
	2 & 4	**LHC** 31 38 **W**	♩ ♪
	3	**D2**	c on 4 instead of c on 3
28	1 & 2	**LHC** 31 38 **W**	♪ ♩ ♪ ♪ ♩
	3 & 4		as above
29	1	**D2**	*(notation)*
	1 & 2	**LHC** 31 38 **W**	♪ ♩ ♪ ♩ ♩
	4	**LHC** 31 38 **W**	♩ ♪ ♩
30	1 & 2	**LHC** 31 38 **W**	♩ ♩ ♪ ♪ ♩ ♩
	2	**JP**	*(notation)*
31	1	**JP**	*(notation)*
32		**W**	*(notation)*
	1	**D2**	a on 7 added, c on 5 deleted
	3	**D2**	a on 7 added
	4	**D2**	e on 4, c on 6 and a on 7 added
	3 & 4 38		*(notation)*

33	3	**W**	a on 2 omitted
35	4	**LHC W**	
38	1	**W**	b on 3 omitted
40	1	**JP**	
42	3	**D2 JP**	b on 4 and c on 5 omitted
43	1 & 2	**38**	
44	1 & 2	**38**	
47	1	**JP 31 LHC**	c on 4 omitted
		38	b on 3 omitted
48	2	**38**	d on 2, f on 3, d on 6
49–50		**W**	

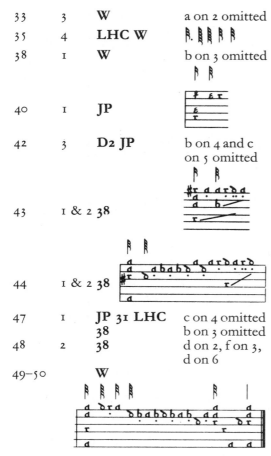

To give some idea of the treatment found in versions that do not conform to the accepted pattern, here are some quotations from other English sources:

Bars 1–8   **30** f. 14v.

Bars 9–16   **FD**

Bars 9–16   **WB**

Bars 25–32   **D2** ff. 75v/77

16. **D5** ff. 47v/48. WT. "J: Dowlande".
This pavan, though opening with the "Lachrimæ" theme, does not, in its development, resemble any of the pieces in **LoST**.
Bar 48

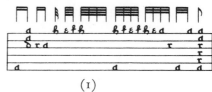

(1)

(1) Notes obliterated.

17. **D5** ff. 64v/65. "The Lady Russells Pauen". Anon.

D9 ff. 5v/6. "The Lady Russells paven".
Anon.
G ff. 37v/38. WT. Anon.
30 ff. 5v/6. "A Pauen by John Dowlande".
All have the diapason at D.

D5, D9 and **G** all share a number of mistakes, even to the incorrect time marks and anomalous barring of strain 3 and the inconsistency of the bass and the consecutive octaves of bars 36 and 44. **30** avoids some of these errors but introduces various others, mostly by the omission of essential notes and the addition of some inessential ones.

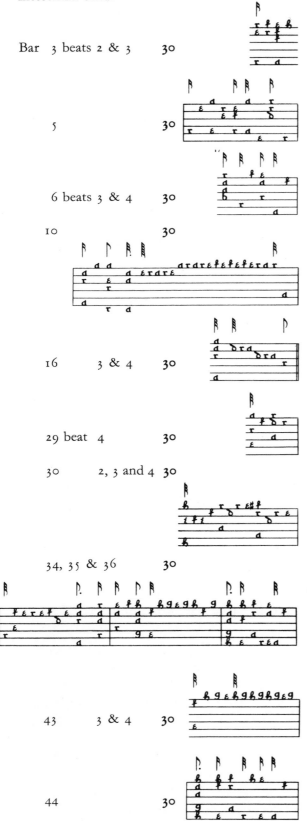

Bar 3 beats 2 & 3   30

5   30

6 beats 3 & 4   30

10   30

16   3 & 4   30

29 beat 4   30

30   2, 3 and 4   30

34, 35 & 36   30

43   3 & 4   30

44   30

47 & 48   30

18. **D5** ff. 51v/52. WT. "JD".
D9 ff. 1v/2. WT. "JD. B of Musicke".
Both have the diapason at D.

19. **D2** f. 53. WT. Anon.
D5 ff. 21v/10. WT. Anon.
H f. 11. WT. Anon. A B C only.
31 ff. 28v/29. "maister pypers galiard by maister Dowland". Diapason at D.
G f. 28v. WT. Anon. Diapason at D.
D9 f. 73v. WT. Anon. Diapason at D.
30 ff. 3v/4. "The galliard to the pauan before". Diapason at D.
BTH f. 107v. "Galliarda Ioannis Doland". Diapason at D.
LoST No. 18. "Captaine Digorie Piper his Galiard". The only source for Piper's full name.
Bk. 1 No. IV. "If my complaints could passions move".
There are two distinct settings of this piece:

1. **D2, D5, 31** and **G.** This is the earlier version, for a six-course lute, except in **31** and **G** where in each case, the seventh course is added in one place.

2. **30** and **D9,** for a seven-course lute throughout. It seems unlikely that **30** is a genuine Dowland setting. It is, however, included as No. 89, where the reasons for this opinion are stated in the notes.

Bar 5 last note   There is great divergence of opinion in the sources:
     D2, D5   d on 3
     D9, G, 31, H   d on 2 **LoST** has F in the 2nd treble viol.
     30   e on 2
     BTH   omits the note in the inner voice and gives f on 1, agreeing with the lute part in **LoST**

Bar 18 beat 1   **D5 & 31**

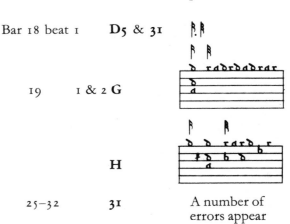

19   1 & 2 **G**

H

25–32   **31**   A number of errors appear

all through
this division.

20. **D2** f. 7v. "Dowlands Galliard".
Thy f. 22. "Douwlants Gailliarde".
This is one of three closely related pieces of which No. 33 and No. 40 are the other two. All contain material derived from the 16th-century *genre* of compositions in which the sounds of battle were imitated. Although the phrases used by Dowland were also incorporated into works by a number of other composers they are not directly derived from the two best-known examples of these onomatopœic compositions: Clement Jannequin's "La Bataille" or "La Guerre", written to commemorate the Battle of Marignano, fought in 1515; and "Die Schlacht vor Pavia" or "La Battaglia Taliana" by Matthias Werrecore, first printed in 1544. Other compositions for the lute, all anonymous, which contain similar phrases include an untitled piece in **D2** ff. 29v/31; "the Battle" in **FD** ff. 14v/21v; and an arrangement for two lutes, "the battell", in **JP** ff. 52v/53 and 53v/54.

Bar 19 beats 2 & 3 **Thy**

22 & 23   **D2** gives the following reading:

but that of **Thy** seems preferable

Tol f. 6v. "A Galliard by Dowla". This MS gives a somewhat different reading:

21. **D2** f. 56. WT. "J:dowl".
H f. 11v. WT. Anon.
Myn f. 1. "John Dowlands Galliarde".
27 f. [6v]. "Capit[ain] Candishe his Galy[ard]". Anon.

Bar 1   27

5 beat 3   e on 4 instead of c on 2

6   1

9   3   a on 3 added
10   mostly destroyed
11   3   d on 3 and a on 4 added
12   1   a on 2 and b on 3 omitted
13   1   d on 2 omitted
       2 2nd q.   c on 4 omitted
14   1 2nd note   b on 2
15   2   a on 5 added

22. **D2** f. 95. "Dowlands Galliarde". This is one of several interesting examples in **D2** in which the scribe has first written the piece for a six-course lute and subsequently has altered it for a seven-course lute with the diapason at D. It is clear that the diapason is intended to replace the higher octave and not to be played with it, although the scribe has, in fact, omitted to score through or erase the upper note, except in bar 11. The three following versions give A B C only and are for a six-course lute.
D2 f. 56. WT. Anon.
D2 f. 60. "Dow. Galliard".
G f. 23. WT. Anon.
The title "Dowland's First Galliard" is taken from the C.U.L. Consort Books:
Dd. 5. 21, f. 5v (Recorder). "Dowlands first galliarde".
Dd. 5. 20, f. 5 (Bass viol). "Dowlands first galliarde".
Dd. 14. 24, f. 34v (Cittern). "Dowlands 1 Galliarde".
Bars 34 to 42   **D2** f. 60.

23. **D2** f. 93. "The frogg galliard". Anon.
D2 f. 40. WT. Anon. A B only. A very simple setting.
G ff. 26v/27. WT. Anon.
23a. **FD** f. 12v. "frog Galliard Jo:dowlande".

Autograph. Diapason at D.

30 ff. 42v/43. "Frogg galliard". Anon. Diapason at D. Probably not by Dowland.

Thy f. 28v. "Frogge Gaillarde". Anon. A B only.

Bk. 1 No. VI. "Now, O now I needs must part".

NGC p. 54. "Nou, Nou". Anon. In F. Lacks the characteristic changes of rhythm of the genuine Dowland settings.

Nür f.9v. 'galliarda Frog Canto'; f.10 'galliarda Frog Pasy'.

It is possible the tune was not originally composed by Dowland. Only one of the five settings in the English MS sources has his name attached, and this may refer only to the lute setting and divisions. Morley also included an arrangement in his *Consort Lessons* (1599 and 1611) and, though Morley was careless in the matter of attributions, it is noticeable that he did not place this galliard in the group of pieces known to be by Dowland. The tune also appears in the ballad repertoire. Two versions are given in the transcriptions: the anonymous setting of **D2** f. 93 and **G** which has many characteristics to suggest Dowland as the composer, and the version from **FD** to which his autograph is added. The setting from **30** is included among the unlikely attributions (No. 92), with reasons for its rejection.

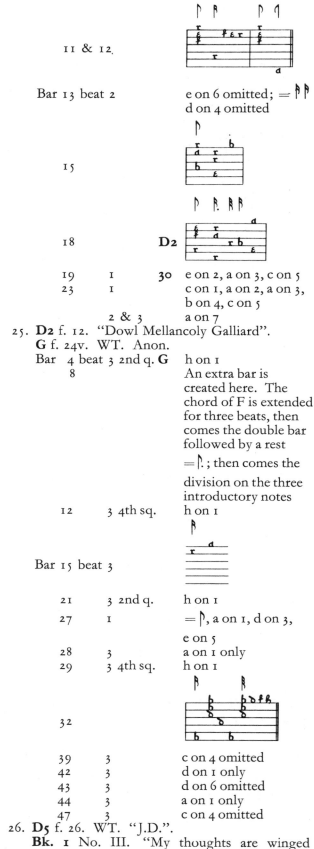

Bar 11 beat 1   **G**

30	3	
32	2	
54	3	
63	3	

24. D2 f. 58. "fr. Dac. Galliard". Anon.
Richard Newton suggests this curious title may be an erroneous contraction of the name K. Darcy. The supposition is supported by the fact that the piece is immediately preceded by "K. Darcies Spirite" and followed on the other side of the folio by "K. Darcyes Galliard".

30 f. 33v. "Galliard J. D.". Diapason at D.

Bk. 1 No. XIX. "Awake sweet loue thou art returnd".

Bar	1 beat 1	**30** a on 7 instead of h on 6
	4	3 a on 1
	6	omitted
	9	3 2nd q. a on 5
	10	2

11 & 12	

Bar 13 beat 2	e on 6 omitted; d on 4 omitted

15	

18	**D2**

19	1	**30** e on 2, a on 3, c on 5
23	1	c on 1, a on 2, a on 3, b on 4, c on 5
	2 & 3	a on 7

25. D2 f. 12. "Dowl Mellancoly Galliard". **G** f. 24v. WT. Anon.

Bar	4 beat 3 2nd q.	**G** h on 1
	8	An extra bar is created here. The chord of F is extended for three beats, then comes the double bar followed by a rest; then comes the division on the three introductory notes
	12	3 4th sq. h on 1

Bar 15 beat 3	

21	3 2nd q.	h on 1
27	1	a on 1, d on 3, e on 5
28	3	a on 1 only
29	3 4th sq.	h on 1
32		
39	3	c on 4 omitted
42	3	d on 1 only
43	3	d on 6 omitted
44	3	a on 1 only
47	3	c on 4 omitted

26. D5 f. 26. WT. "J.D.".

Bk. 1 No. III. "My thoughts are winged with hopes".

LoST No. 13. "Sir John Souch his galliard". Several instances of characteristic word-painting suggest the vocal form may have preceded the instrumental galliard. The text of **D5** is not entirely satisfactory and may have been an arrangement by Holmes himself since it exists nowhere else. Some of the obvious errors can be corrected by comparison with **Bk. 1** and **LoST**.

27. D5 f. 49v. WT. "J.D.".

28. **D5** ff. 35v/36. WT. "J.D.". Diapason at D.
G ff. 20v/21. WT. Anon. Diapason at D.
LHC ff. 54v/55. Galliarda. J:D:". Diapasons at F, E♭.
K10 ff. 94v/95. "Galliard Dullande". Diapasons at F, E♭.
38 ff. 15v/16. "A gallyard upon the gallyard before by Mr Dowland". Diapasons at F, E, D, C.
Profusely marked with ornament signs, fingering points and hold marks.
TGG p. 109. "Galliard 2". "incerti Authoris".
In **38** this galliard follows immediately after a galliard by Daniel Bacheler, composed upon the first four bars of his song "To plead my faith", No. VI of **MB**. There is no further resemblance between the galliard and the song. Besardus (**BTH** f. 120v) mistakenly attributes Bacheler's galliard to Dowland.

Bar 9   **D5 38 LHC** An extra bar is interpolated after bar 9. This appears to be an alternative end to the first strain which, in these MSS, has been written to follow on.
    G K10 TGG Bar 9 of **D5** is omitted and the alternative bar is used. It varies between the different sources:

D5

38

LHC

G

K10 TGG

8 & 17 last beat
TGG

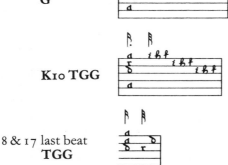

14 last note	f on 2
26 beat 1	dotted rhythm omitted
26 **LHC**	dotted rhythm throughout
32–35 **TGG**	dotted rhythm omitted

Bar 51 beat 1

29. **D5** ff. 16v/17. WT. "J.D.".
LHC f. 10. "Gagliarda J: Doulande". The lute part from **LoST** No. 15. "M. Giles Hobies Galiard".
30. **D5** ff. 25v/26. WT. "Jo:D". Diapason at D.
31. **D5** f. 37. WT. "J:D.". Diapason at D.
D2 f. 82v. WT. Anon.
32. **D9** f. 20. "Mrs vaux Galliarde Jo Dowland Bacheler of Musicke".
TGG p. 108. "Galliardo 1". "incerti Authoris". This version contains a number of errors as well as some genuine variants. It provides an acceptable reading for bar 27 which, in **D9**, is hopelessly confused.

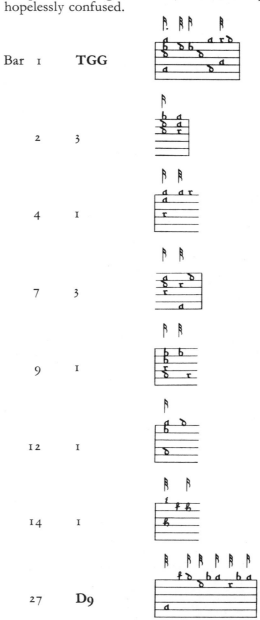

Bar 1   **TGG**
2   3
4   1
7   3
9   1
12   1
14   1
27   **D9**

33. **D9** ff. 17v/18. "Mr Langtons galliard Mr Dow Bach. of Mus.". Diapason at D.
G f. 18v. WT. Anon. Diapason at D.
This galliard is of irregular form—AA' B, with rather more than half of B repeated. See note to 20.
34. **D9** f. 29. "Mignarda Jo Dowlande".

It is possible the divisions are not by Dowland. They are included here, however, as being, if not by Dowland, at least an interesting example of the manner in which a contemporary player would treat his music. In all three MSS there are a number of errors in common which suggests they may have derived from the same source, possibly one which reached the writer in the form of staff notation since he appears to have had great difficulty with the accidentals, especially in the case of D♯.

D2 f. 77. "Mignarde". Anon. A B C only. Diapason at D.

D5 f. 31v. WT. "J.D.". A B C only. Diapason at D.

LoST Galliard No. 14. "M. Henry Noel his Galliard". A B C only.

PS No. V. "Shall I strive with words to move." In the notes bars are numbered to equal those of **D9**.

Bar 7 beat 1 2nd q. **D2** and **D5** both give f on 2. Either reading can be justified from **LoST** but f on 2 would belong to the cantus voice and would break the continuity of the altus

19	**D2**	Dotted rhythm throughout the bar
	D5	Dotted rhythm omitted
23	**D2**	Dotted rhythm throughout the bar

35. **D9** f. 37v. "Galliard J Dow   de". The 4th, 5th and 6th letters of the name have been destroyed by damp.

Thy f. 26v. "Gallarde". Anon.

Bars are twice the normal length, i.e., they contain six beats in each. A B C only.

36. **D9** f. 19v. "Mr Knights Galliard J. Dowla". Diapason at D.

D5 f. 56. "Mr knights galliard Jo Dowland". Diapason at D.

Bar 4 beat 2   **D5**   Dotted rhythm omitted

37. **Bk. 1** No. XXII. "My Lord Chamberlaine his galliard". Diapason at D.

After the first printing in 1597 further editions of the *First Booke of Songes* were issued in 1600, 1603, 1606 and 1613. W. C. Hazlitt, in his *Hand-Book to the Popular, Poetical and Dramatic Literature of Great Britain* (1867), p. 163, gives a printing of 1608. A reprint of this date is also mentioned by A. B. Grosart in *The Works . . . of Fulke Greville, Lord Brooke* (1870). No copy of this edition is, however, known to be extant today. A number of alterations and corrections were made in this composition between the first printing and the edition of 1613.

38. **MB.** "The Right Honourable the Lord Viscount Lisle, His Galliard". Called in the Table of Contents "Sir Robert Sidney's Galliard". An odd mistake since he was created Viscount Lisle on May 4th, 1605, and **MB** was not printed until 1610. Diapasons at D and C.

The opening phrase is taken from the setting by Orlando de Lassus of the famous *chanson spirituelle*, "Suzanne un jour". For an earlier version of this piece, called "Susanna Galliard", see No. 91.

LoST No. 19. "M. Bucton's Galliard". A B C only. The lute part bears little resemblance to the solo version.

39. **FD** f. 6. "Doulands rounde battell galyarde". This piece may have been played as a solo, but it fits very convincingly with the remaining consort parts in the C.U.L. Consort Books:

Dd. 5. 21, f. 5v (Recorder).
Dd. 5. 20, f. 5 (Bass Viol).
Dd. 14. 24 f. 36v (Cittern).

40. **Var** Galliard No. 1. "The most high and mightie *Christianus* the fourth King of Denmark, his Galliard". Diapasons at F and D. See Note to No. 20.

This is a final and revised version that Dowland evidently prepared for publication. The last eight bars, in the form in which they appear in **Var** are not found in any other source.

D9 f. 23. This folio contains the first 48 bars followed by the subscription "Mr. Mildmays Galliard J.D."

f. 94v contains bar 49 to the end, followed by the subscription "Dowlands plus in prima p[arte libri]". Mr. Richard Newton has suggested the conclusion of the Latin words which, in the MS are destroyed.

FD ff. 10v/11. "the Battell gallyard Mr Dowland". Diapason at D.

JP ff. 17v/18. "the battell galyerd mr dowlande". Diapason at D.

W f. 5v. "The Battle Galliard". Anon. Diapason at D.

38 ff. 12v/13. "The Battle galliard Mr Dowland". Diapasons at F, E and D.

Tol f. 7v. "The bataille Galliarde by Johnson". Diapason at D.

TGG pp. 112/113. "galliarda Robert. Doulandt". Diapasons at F and D.

This is full of misprints and should not be treated as a source.

LoST. Galliard No. 1. A B C only.

Bar 15 & 16   **D9 W 38**

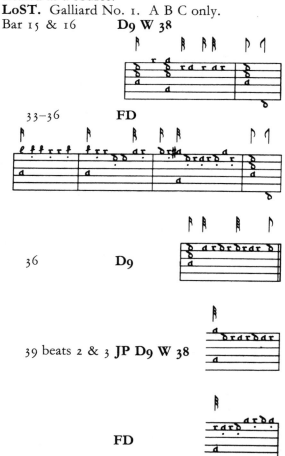

33–36   **FD**

36   **D9**

39 beats 2 & 3 **JP D9 W 38**

FD

326

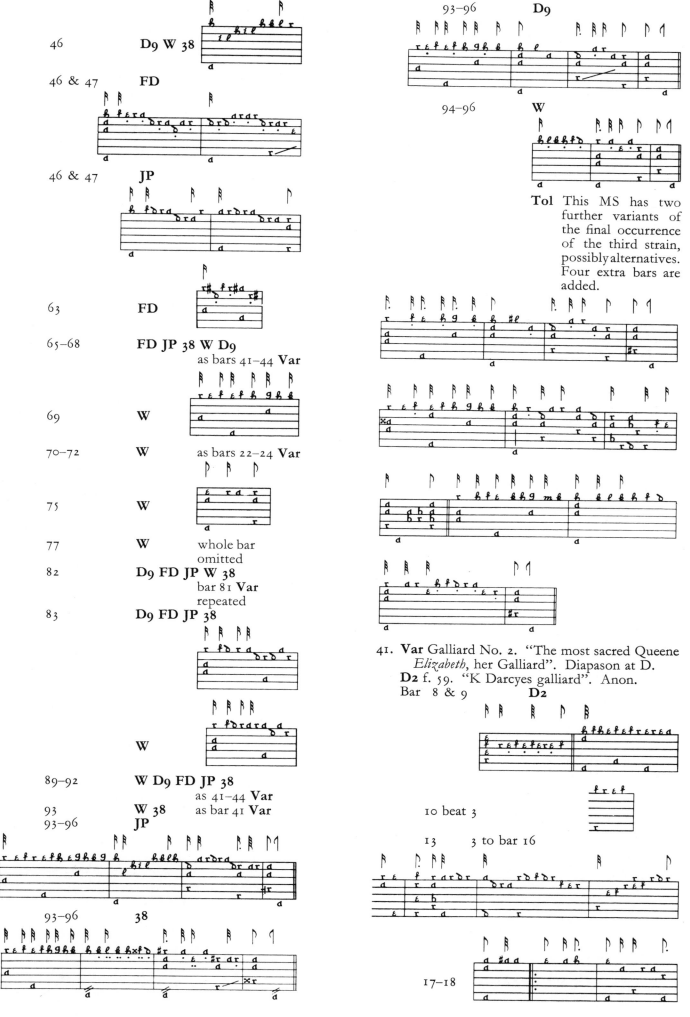

46   **D9 W 38**

46 & 47   **FD**

46 & 47   **JP**

63   **FD**

65–68   **FD JP 38 W D9**
as bars 41–44 **Var**

69   **W**

70–72   **W**   as bars 22–24 **Var**

75   **W**

77   **W**   whole bar omitted

82   **D9 FD JP W 38**   bar 81 **Var** repeated

83   **D9 FD JP 38**

W

89–92   **W D9 FD JP 38**   as 41–44 **Var**

93   **W 38**   as bar 41 **Var**

93–96   **JP**

93–96   **38**

93–96   **D9**

94–96   **W**

Tol This MS has two further variants of the final occurrence of the third strain, possibly alternatives. Four extra bars are added.

41. **Var** Galliard No. 2. "The most sacred Queene *Elizabeth*, her Galliard". Diapason at D.
D2 f. 59. "K Darcyes galliard". Anon.
Bar 8 & 9   **D2**

10 beat 3

13   3 to bar 16

17–18

327

18 beat 1   e on 1 can hardly be a mistake since it occurs again in bar 26

31 beat 3 to end

42. **FD** f. 16. "Can she excuse J:doulande". The signature is in Dowland's own hand.

G f. 24. WT. Anon.

WB No. 12. "A Galliarde by I.D.". A B C only. (Orpharion).

H f. 11v. WT. Anon. A B C only.

D2 f. 40v. WT. Anon; f. 62v. WT. Anon. A B C only.

30 f. 48. WT. Anon. See No. 90.

K10 f. 2. "Gagliarda". Anon; f. 2v. WT. Anon. First strain only. f. 56v. "daulant gagliarde". All poor settings.

Thy f. 22v. "Can she excuse". Anon. A B C only.

Nür f. 6v. "Galliard Pipers No. 1". Anon. The first bar is unrecognisable as either "Piper's Galliard" or "Can she excuse", but the latter piece is obviously intended and the theme of "The woods so wild" is incorporated.

Nür f. ?. "Galliard Pipers No. 2". Anon. Another attempt to write "Can she excuse" which is slightly more successful.

Nür f. 65v. "Galliarta Pipers". Anon. Again "Can she excuse" but very inaccurate.

B f. 30. "Galliarda". Anon.

B f. 124. "Galliarda". Anon.

SdM pp. 36/37/38. "Galiarde du comte Essex". A long and elaborate setting probably by Nicolas Vallet.

TGG p. 47. "Galliarda 12". "incerti Authoris", followed by Variations by Valentinus Strobelius.

LoST No. 12. "The Earl of Essex Galliard". A B C only.

Bk. 1 No. V. "Can she excuse my wrongs with vertues cloake". See also 42a.

The authentic versions of this piece fall into two distinct groups:

1. **FD** and **G** have divisions which, though not identical, are worked on much the same plan. **H** and **D2**, though consisting of A B C only, share the characteristic of having eight bars in B. **LoST** also falls into this group.

2. **Var** and **WB** both have nine bars in B.

N6 f. 37. WT. Anon. A consort part. Sidney Beck includes it in his edition of Morley's *First Booke of Consort Lessons* 1599 & 1611 (1959) but its use with Morley's arrangement involves the addition of accidentals in some of the other instrumental parts.

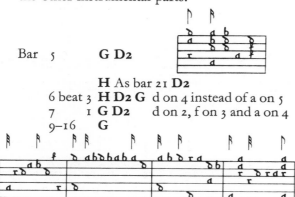

Bar 5   **G D2**

H As bar 21 **D2**

6 beat 3 **H D2 G** d on 4 instead of a on 5

7   1 **G D2**   d on 2, f on 3 and a on 4

9–16   **G**

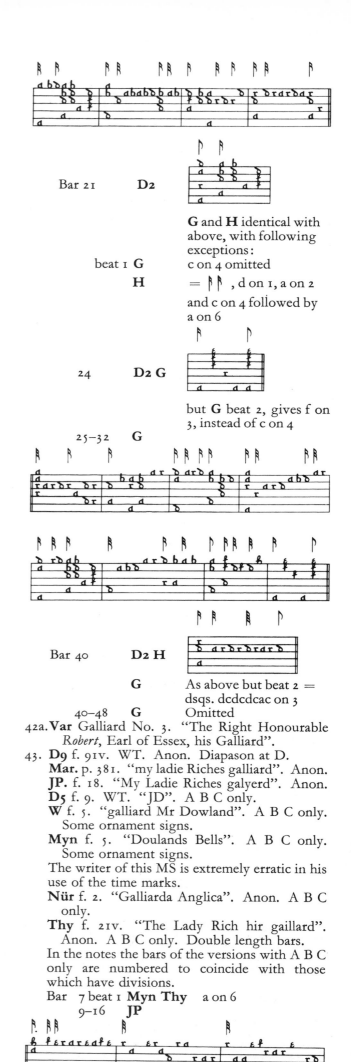

Bar 21   **D2**

G and **H** identical with above, with following exceptions:

beat 1 **G**   c on 4 omitted

H   = , d on 1, a on 2 and c on 4 followed by a on 6

24   **D2 G**

but **G** beat 2, gives f on 3, instead of c on 4

25–32   **G**

Bar 40   **D2 H**

G   As above but beat 2 = dsqs. dcdcdcac on 3

40–48   **G**   Omitted

42a. **Var** Galliard No. 3. "The Right Honourable *Robert*, Earl of Essex, his Galliard".

43. **D9** f. 91v. WT. Anon. Diapason at D.

Mar. p. 381. "my ladie Riches galliard". Anon.

JP. f. 18. "My Ladie Riches galyerd". Anon.

D5 f. 9. WT. "JD". A B C only.

W f. 5. "galliard Mr Dowland". A B C only. Some ornament signs.

Myn f. 5. "Doulands Bells". A B C only. Some ornament signs.

The writer of this MS is extremely erratic in his use of the time marks.

Nür f. 2. "Galliarda Anglica". Anon. A B C only.

Thy f. 21v. "The Lady Rich hir gaillard". Anon. A B C only. Double length bars.

In the notes the bars of the versions with A B C only are numbered to coincide with those which have divisions.

Bar 7 beat 1 **Myn Thy**   a on 6

9–16   **JP**

Bar 9–16   **Mar**

Bar 19 beat 1 **D5 Thy**   a on 6
  20–24   **Mar**

  20–24   **JP**

  25–32   **JP**

  25–32   **Mar**

Bar 35 beat 1 **D5**   dotted rhythm omitted

Bar 35 beat 2 **D5 JP W**   d on 2
            Mar Thy W   whole bar dotted rhythm
  37 & 39 beat 1 **D5**   dotted rhythm omitted

  39   **JP**

  41–48   **JP**

  41–48   **Mar**

43a. Var Galliard No. 5. "The Right Honourable the Lady Rich, her Galliard". Diapason at D. This version embodies Dowland's final revisions of the piece.

44. N6 f. 2. "The Erle of Darbies Galiard by Mr Jo Dowland". Diapason at D.
  N6 f. 1. WT. Anon. Diapason at D.
  G f. 21. WT. Anon. A B C only. Diapason at D.
  W f. 7. "Galliard Dowlande". A B C only. Diapason at D.
  Tol f. 13v. "a galiarde by Mr Dowland". Diapason at D.
  D5 f. 38. WT. Anon. A B C only. Diapason at D.
  The copy on f. 1 of **N6** is full of errors. The writer himself appears to have been dissatisfied and to have rewritten the piece on f. 2. No variants will therefore be given from f. 1.

Bar 4, 5 & 6   **W**   There is confusion in the tablature. Although the scribe has added a bar, at the end of the line, for insertion, he is still one bar short

Bar 4   **Tol W**   As in **Var**

  5   **Tol**

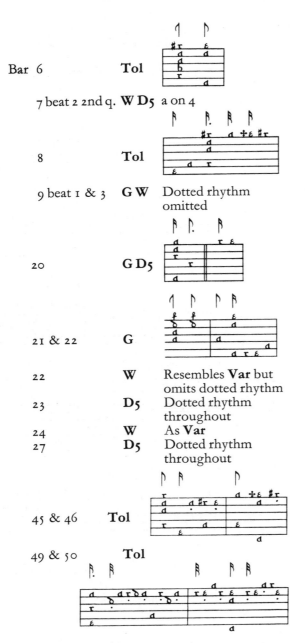

Bar 6   **Tol**

7 beat 2 2nd q.   **W D5** a on 4

8   **Tol**

9 beat 1 & 3   **G W**   Dotted rhythm omitted

20   **G D5**

21 & 22   **G**

22   **W**   Resembles **Var** but omits dotted rhythm

23   **D5**   Dotted rhythm throughout

24   **W**   As **Var**

27   **D5**   Dotted rhythm throughout

45 & 46   **Tol**

49 & 50   **Tol**

44a. Var Galliard No. 4. "The Right Honourable *Ferdinando* Earle of Darby, his Galliard". Diapasons at F and D.

This is the only version in which the dotted rhythm is employed for the three introductory notes. In the B.M. copy the whole of the bottom of the page, from immediately below the sixth line of the lowest line of tablature has been cut away, and in bar 58, beat 2, a on 6 is missing. The Bodleian Library copy is, however, perfect.

45. Var Galliard No. 6. "The Right Honorable the Lady *Cliftons* Spirit". Diapason at D.
Attributed to Robert Dowland. The identity of A B C of this piece with "K. Darcies Spirite" of **D2**, which must have been written before 1591, and the characteristic style of the divisions, leave no doubt that the composer was John.
D2 f. 58. "K. Darcies Spirite J:Dowl".

Bar 8   **D2**

46. PS No. XXII. "Galliard to Lachrimæ". Diapasons at F, E♭ and D.

47. Var Almain No. 7. "Sir John Smith his Almaine". Anon.
The anomalous form of this piece is very curious. It is based on a theme of two eight-bar strains. In the first 32 bars each strain is stated and is then followed by the division. The arrangement may be shown thus:

Strain	A	A'	B	B'
Bars	1–8	9–16	17–24	25–32

This double statement then becomes the theme for a further set of divisions, and may be shown thus:

Strain	A2	A2'	B2	B2'
Bars	33–40	41–48	49–56	57–64

but on examining strain B' it will be seen there is no division on the first two bars of strain B (bars 17–18) and that the third and fourth bars of strain B (bars 19–20) are varied twice over (bars 25–26 and 27–28).
Strain B2' is arranged in the same way. There is no division on bars 17–18, but bars 19–20 are varied twice over (bars 57–58, 59–60).
This irregular form might be dismissed as a series of mistakes were it not that other sources confirm the pattern.
FD ff. 13v/14. "Mr Smythes Allmon Jo. Doulande".
The signature is in Dowland's own hand. There are a number of minor variants but the whole lay-out is identical with **Var**. A number of vital notes in the bass are omitted.
Mar p. 384. "An almayne douland".
The bars are double the length of those in **Var**. AA' BB' only. In B' the division is arranged in the same curious pattern. The piece contains a great number of errors and it seems unlikely the rather undistinguished divisions are by Dowland.
27 f. [10]. "Smith Almain". Anon.
First section and beginning of division only.
B f. 43. "Almande Angl.". Anon.
A short and incorrect version of three strains only.
Thy f. 503. "Allemand Angloyse". Anon.
Bar length as in **Mar**. A BB only, but the repeat of B begins at the second bar and consists of three bars only. A poor text.

Bar 24 beat 4   **FD** c on 1 and c on 2 added

54   3 & 4

61

62 last note   d on 2

47a. 38 f. 8v. "Smythes Allmayne". Anon. Diapasons at F and D.
This is the only version in which B' is a straight division on B. There is no proof that this setting is by Dowland but the single line arrangement of the divisions is similar to that of No. 48a, to which he signed his name. At first sight these two settings suggest they might be consort parts, single parts of duets or arrangements to play with a bass viol, but comparison with the bass of each strain will

show that the divisions do not fit over an exact repetition.

48. **D2** f. 48. "Allmaine J. Dowland".
   Wi f. 17. "ane almane". Anon.
   W f. 5. "Almayne Dowland". No bar lines; double bars at the end of each section.
   These three versions all have the strains arranged in the following order: A B C D E D.
   Myn f. 10. "Doulands allman". Bars half the length of **D2**.
   Strains arranged in the following order: AA′ BB′ D E D. C is omitted altogether. The time marks are erratic and there are many errors in the notation.
   27 f. [10v]. Fragment only.
   Thy ff. 492/493. "Mr Daulants allmande". Bar length as in **D2**.
   Four versions which may be a rather crude arrangement for a quartet of lutes at different pitches.
   L p. 347. "Chorea Anglica 5". Anon. In F with diapason at F.
   A B E D. C omitted. Very inaccurate.
   L p. 491. "Almanda Dulandi". In F.
   A and B only.
   TGG p. 80. "Chorea Anglica". Anon. In F.
   Very inaccurate. It is almost impossible to discover the arrangement of the strains.
   DM f. 59. "Ballet Englese". "Incerto". In F.
   AA′ BB′. Diapason at F.
   Following bar 4 **Myn** gives:

   Following bar 8 **Myn** gives:

   This is full of confusion and an extra bar has been added.

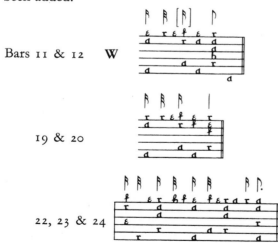

   Bars 11 & 12 **W**

   19 & 20

   22, 23 & 24

48a.**FD** f. 11v. "the Lady Laitons Almone Jo: doulande".
   The signature is in Dowland's own hand. Diapason at D.
   BTH f. 139v. "Chorea Anglicana Doolandi". Six courses only. Wherever the seventh appears in **FD** c on 5 is substituted. It is almost identical in other respects with **FD**, but E is

omitted and the sections run AA′ BB′ CC′ DD′. The barring is very erratic.
   Bar 16 **BTH**

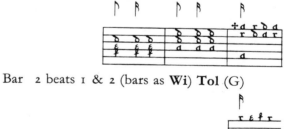

   23 beat 2 & 24 **BTH**

49. **D2** f. 38. WT. "Jo: Dowlande".
   D2 f. 47. WT. "J.D.".
   Identical with above except that at bar 12 the double bar has been taken as the bar line and an extra bar has been made at the end, by taking the G major chord as the first beat of the bar and breaking it to fill the four beats.

50. **Wi** f. 15. "Mistris Whittes thinge Jhone Dowlande".
   D2 f. 63v. "W Thinge". A B C only.
   Tol f. 7. "Mrs Whites Choyce". Anon.
   This version differs from all others in having the first two beats on the dominant chord. Bars are half-length and there are many variants. It is probably an arrangement by the writer of the MS.
   27 f. [6]. WT. Anon. Incomplete.
   JP f. 19. WT. Anon. AA′ BB′ CC′.
   So much altered that it can hardly rank as a genuine source.
   38 f. 2. "Mrs Whites Choyse". Anon. AA′ BB′ CC′.
   In F, but otherwise almost identical with **Wi**.
   Tol f. 7. "Mrs Whites Choice". Anon.
   In F. Another very individual setting which has many harmonic variants from the more generally accepted form. It begins:

   Bar 2 beats 1 & 2 (bars as **Wi**) Tol (G)

   4 & 5 **Tol** (G)

   9 & 10 **Tol** (G)

51. **D5** f. 32. WT. "J.D.". Diapason at D.
   This piece is of a curiously irregular structure. It is placed among the almains for lack of a better classification.

52. **D2** f. 100v. WT. Anon. Title from **LoST**.
   G f. 24. WT. Anon.
   Bars half the length of **D2**.
   B f. 46v. "Dolandi Saltarella".
   Bars as in **G**. First four bars, then as **D2**.
   Closely resembles text of **G**.
   DM f. 58. "Almande Ioan Douland".
   The lute part from **LoST**. The tune is absent
   and this should not be treated as a solo version.
   LoST No. 20. "Mistresse Nichols Almand".

   Bar 2 beat 3   **G** b on 4 added
     3   4   a on 1 and e on 5
     4   1   c on 5 as bass

     8   3 & 4

     9 & 10

     10   1   According to **LoST** the
                 melody note would be
                 A, but both **D2** and **B**
                 give c on 2

     10, 11 & 12   **B**

53. **FD** f. 23v. WT. Anon. Bars 1 to 8 only. In
   Dowland's hand. Diapason at D.
   D9 f. 28v. "Mrs Cliftons Allmaine Jo Dowland". Diapason at D.
   G f. 44. WT. Anon. Bars half length. A B
   only. Diapason at D.
   Since Dowland wrote no more than the first
   eight bars in **FD** the remainder has been added
   from **D9**. The variant reading of bars 1–8 of **D9**
   is given below:

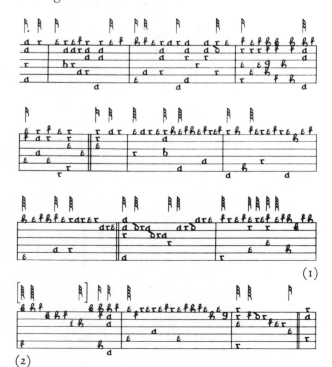

(1)

(2)

(1) Bar line omitted.
(2) Time marks between brackets have values
   doubled.
G agrees with **D9** but with the following
variants:

Bar 3 beats 3 & 4 **G**

     10

54. **D5** f. 7. WT. Anon. Title from **64**. Diapason
   at D.
   FD f. 22v. "my Lady Hunsdons Allmande
   Jo: doulande Bacheler of musick".
   The whole composition is written in Dowland's
   own hand. At the end he has added his
   signature and degree. Curiously this is a much
   less satisfactory text than that of **D5**; possibly
   an early version. AA' B C D C. Diapason at D.
   64 f. 1v. "My lady hunssdons puffe Douland".
   Bars half the length of **D5** and **FD**. AA' B C D.
   Diapason at D.
   D9 f. 38. WT. "J. Dowland".
   Bars as in **64**. A B C D. Diapason at D.
   Bar 2 beat 3 (bars counted as **D5**)
                     D9 Dotted rhythm
                           omitted
              3 & 4 (bars counted as **D5**)

     64

   Bar 3 beat 4 final sq. **64** c on 2

     4   2   **FD**

     6   1 & 2   **FD**

     7   **FD**

     13   4   **D9 FD 64** =

     15   1 & 2   **FD**

     2   **D9**

     4   **64** =

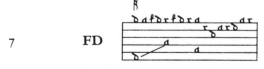

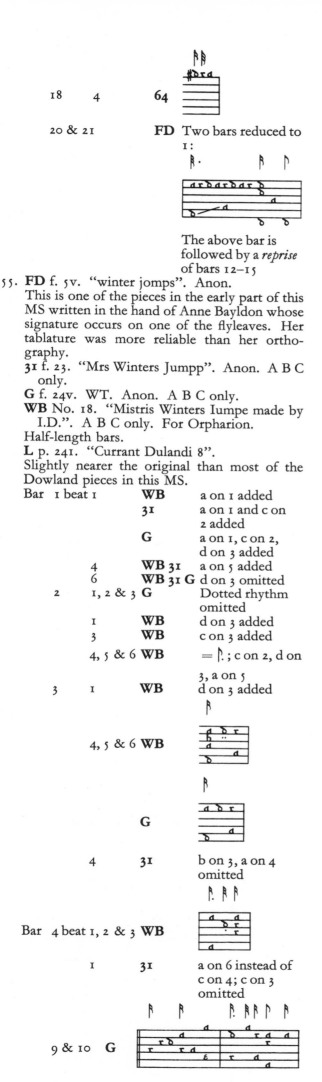

18   4   **64**

20 & 21   **FD**   Two bars reduced to 1:

The above bar is followed by a *reprise* of bars 12–15

55. **FD** f. 5v. "winter jomps". Anon.
This is one of the pieces in the early part of this MS written in the hand of Anne Bayldon whose signature occurs on one of the flyleaves. Her tablature was more reliable than her orthography.
31 f. 23. "Mrs Winters Jumpp". Anon. A B C only.
G f. 24v. WT. Anon. A B C only.
WB No. 18. "Mistris Winters Iumpe made by I.D.". A B C only. For Orpharion. Half-length bars.
L p. 241. "Currant Dulandi 8".
Slightly nearer the original than most of the Dowland pieces in this MS.

Bar	beat		
1	1	**WB**	a on 1 added
		31	a on 1 and c on 2 added
		G	a on 1, c on 2, d on 3 added
	4	**WB 31**	a on 5 added
	6	**WB 31 G**	d on 3 omitted
2	1, 2 & 3	**G**	Dotted rhythm omitted
	1	**WB**	d on 3 added
	3	**WB**	c on 3 added
	4, 5 & 6	**WB**	= ♪; c on 2, d on 3, a on 5
3	1	**WB**	d on 3 added
	4, 5 & 6	**WB**	
		G	
	4	**31**	b on 3, a on 4 omitted
Bar 4 beat	1, 2 & 3	**WB**	
	1	**31**	a on 6 instead of c on 4; c on 3 omitted
9 & 10		**G**	

31

9–12 **WB**

11   1   **G**   d on 3 added

12   **G**

15   6   **WB 31**   d on 3 omitted
          G   d on 3, e on 5 omitted
16   1   **WB**   d on 3 added
      3   **WB**   c on 3 added
      4, 5 & 6 **WB**   = ♪; c on 2, d on 3, a on 5

56. **D2** f. 22. "Mrs Whites Nothing Jo Dowland Bacheler of Musicke".

57. **D9** f. 20v. "Mrs vauxes Gigge Jo Dowland Bacheler of Musicke". Diapason at D.

58. **D9** f. 21v. "The Shomakers Wife. A Toy J Dowland". Diapason at F.
D5 f. 6v. WT. Anon. Diapason at F.
The copies are identical except for a few very minor variants. It would be pleasant to be able to establish a connection between this piece and Mrs. Margery Eyre of *The Shoemaker's Holiday* by Thomas Dekker, but, as far as the editors have been able to discover, no such connection exists.

59. **Wi** f. 11. "tarletones riserrectione Jo Dowlande".

60. **N6** f. 21v. "Come away". Anon. Diapason at F.
K10 f. 1v. "Paduana". Anon. Diapason at F.
K10 f. 64v. WT. Anon. In the key of C.
L p. 472. "Commia guinæ Dulandi 5".
L p. 502. "Commia Doulandi".
Bk. 1 No. XVII. "Come againe, sweet loue doth now inuite".
The versions in **K10** and **L** all differ from each other and all are very inaccurate.

61. **D2** f. 55v. "Orlando sleepeth JD".
It is difficult to be sure whether Dowland is the composer or merely the arranger of an already existing piece. His use of the name "Orlando sleepeth" suggests he may have had some particular dramatic situation in mind, and a very appropriate moment occurs in Robert Greene's play *Orlando Furioso*. There is a scene in which Melissa charms Orlando asleep and, according to the stage directions of the 1594 edition, "satyres enter with music and plaie about him, which done they staie, he awaketh and speakes". In support of Dowland as composer is the fact that the earliest known

version, that of **D2**, has his initials attached. On the other hand the seven later versions that have been examined—**BD** "Orlando", **Myn** "Orlando furioso", **Thy** "Orlando", **NS** "Englesa", **TGG** "Orlandus Furiosus", **K10** "Orlando Furioso" and **Flo** "Orlando—Chanson Englesæ"—are all anonymous. It is clear that the tune was well-known on the Continent, although Van den Hove certainly considered that it had its origin in England. In *Shirburn Ballads* (1907), ed. Andrew Clark, No. LVIII is a ballad "My dear adieu! my sweet love, farewell" to "Orlandos musique". The tune, in a somewhat different form, and a bass, are given. In the transcription the value of the time marks has not been halved.

62. **D4** f. 11v. "fortune by Jo:Dowland". Diapason at C.

G f. 27. WT. Anon. Bars double the length of **D4**. Diapason at D.

W f. 2. "Fortune Mr Dowland".

Myn f. 9v. "fortune Douland". Bars as in **G**.

WB No. 6. "Fortune by I.D.".

BD p. 14. "fortune my foe to the consort". Anon.

Thy f. 387. "Fortune Jo Doulande".

An extremely inaccurate version. There are several other settings of this tune in **Thy**, all anon.

This arrangement by Dowland was almost certainly played as a solo, although, as the title in **BD** suggests, it undoubtedly originated as part of a consort. It does not, however, fit the viol, recorder and cittern parts in Dd.5.21, Dd.5.22 and Dd.14.24. Unlike Dowland's solo settings of other ballad tunes the complete melody is never stated.

The tune was exceptionally popular and many settings other than Dowland's are found in the lute MSS and other music books of the period. It was extensively used by ballad writers, particularly for "Lamentations"—ballads purporting to be the last words of notorious criminals—specially written for sale at the public executions. In the transcription the value of the time marks has not been halved.

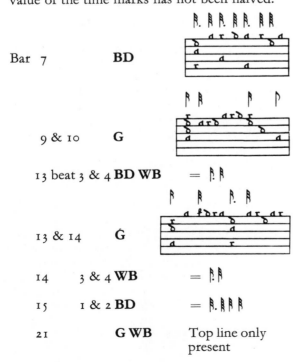

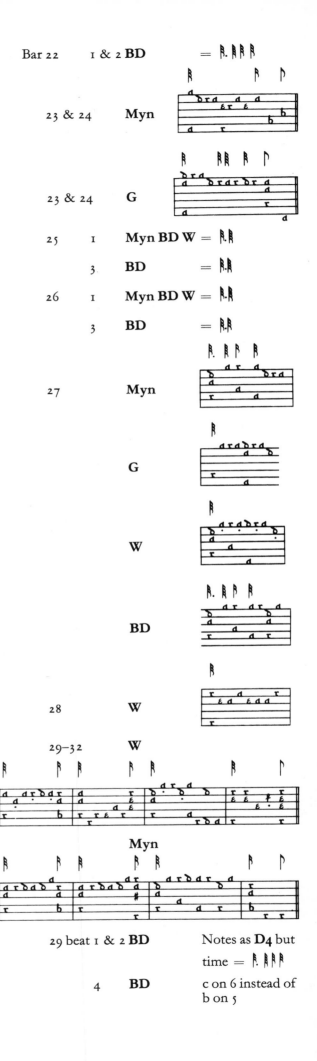

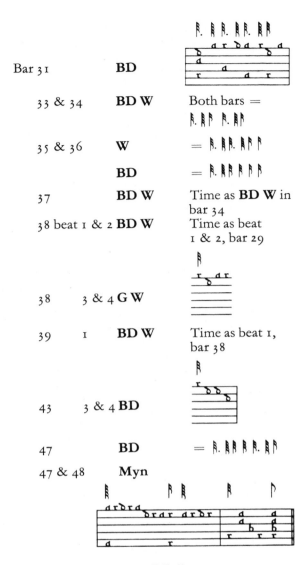

Bar 31   **BD**

33 & 34   **BD W**   Both bars =

35 & 36   **W**   =

         BD   =

37   **BD W**   Time as **BD W** in bar 34

38 beat 1 & 2   **BD W**   Time as beat 1 & 2, bar 29

38   3 & 4 **G W**

39   1   **BD W**   Time as beat 1, bar 38

43   3 & 4 **BD**

47   **BD**   =

47 & 48   **Myn**

63. **D2** f. 56. "Complaint J.D.".

64. **D5** ff. 39v/40. WT. "JD".
Double bars are placed at the end of each four bars.
G ff. 17v/18. WT. Anon.
WB No. 16. "Go from my windowe made by I.D.". (Orpharion).
JP f. 29v. "Go from my window by M Dowland".

Bar 9 beat 4   **G**   f on 2 omitted

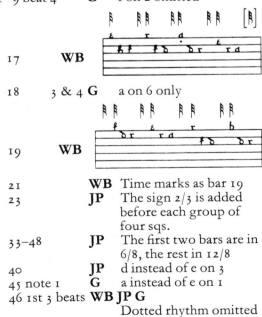

17   **WB**

18   3 & 4 **G**   a on 6 only

19   **WB**

21   **WB**   Time marks as bar 19
23   **JP**   The sign 2/3 is added before each group of four sqs.
33–48   **JP**   The first two bars are in 6/8, the rest in 12/8
40   **JP**   d instead of e on 3
45 note 1   **G**   a instead of e on 1
46 1st 3 beats   **WB JP G**
         Dotted rhythm omitted

---

55 beat 3   **G**   e on 4 instead of g on 5
         JP   g on 5
         WB   b on 4
68   2 2nd note   All sources give a on 1. This curious mistake which gives F double sharp is historically unlikely and musically incorrect in the pattern of the sequence. The most likely explanation of its presence is that it originated as one of the many misprints in Barley and that the extant MS sources are all derived directly or indirectly from the faulty printing. This explanation could also apply to the incorrect F sharp in bar 55, which persisted in all but one source.

65. **D2** f. 58. "Lord Strangs March J.D.".
Although the first bar of this piece is very similar to the opening of "The Earle of Oxfords Marche", also known as "My Lord of Oxenfords Maske", there is no further likeness between the two compositions.

66. **JP** f. 25. "My lord willobes wellcome home by John dowland".
G f. 38. WT. Anon.
D2 f. 58v. "My L Williaghby Tune J.D.".
Bars double length. A very inaccurate version.
Myn f. 1. "Mmy lord wilobie". Anon.
Bars double length.
Wi f. 12. "my lo: willobeis' tune Jhone Doulande".
Bars double length.
This tune appears to have been originally associated with several jigs concerning a character named "Rowland". A "Rowland and the Sexton" was "entered" in 1591, but no copies of an English text are known. A version of the comedy was taken to the Continent by an English troupe of actors, probably under the famous clown Will Kemp, in 1585 and 1586. One, or possibly two, German translations of the piece have survived. The name of Lord Willoughby was almost certainly not associated with the tune until after his return from the Low Countries in 1589 (see Charles Read Baskervill, *The Elizabethan Jig* (1931). It is notable that Byrd (**FVB** No. CLX) still used the title "Rowland". It appears with different names in a number of Continental lute sources: **L** p. 372 "Der Rolandt"; **Fab** p. 9 "Roland"; **NS** f. 21v "Roland"; **Thy** f. 389 "Soet, Soet Robertgen"; **NGC** f. 83 "Soet Robertgen"; **SdM** p. 47 "Soet, soet Robertgen"; **BTH** f. 134 "Allemande".

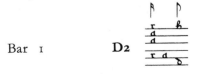

Bar 1   **D2**

2 beat 3   **Wi**   c on 5 added
    4   **D2**   d, f on 1 omitted, c on

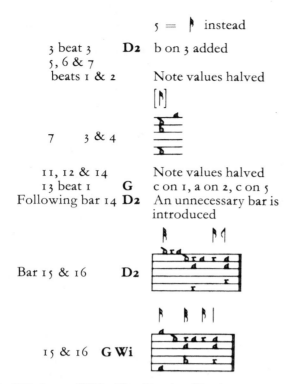

		5 = ♪	instead
3 beat 3	**D2**	b on 3 added	
5, 6 & 7			
beats 1 & 2		Note values halved	
7	3 & 4		
11, 12 & 14		Note values halved	
13 beat 1	**G**	c on 1, a on 2, c on 5	
Following bar 14	**D2**	An unnecessary bar is introduced	
Bar 15 & 16	**D2**		
15 & 16	**G Wi**		

66a. FD f. 9v. WT. "Jo. Douland". Autograph.
Except for a few unimportant details the first 16 bars of this version are identical with "My Lord willoughbies welcome home" of **JP** f. 33v, which in itself appears to be an arrangement of Byrd's virginals piece "Rowland", **FVB** No. CLX.
Tol f. 11v. "My Lo: Wilobies welcom home" by "Jo: Dowland".
This part for a second lute came to light when Robert Spencer acquired the MS from Lord Tollemache in 1965. The **FD** piece is complete in itself and it seems likely that the second part was added later; evidence is lacking to show whether by Dowland himself or by another composer. The time marks consist of staff notation signs, a fact which suggests that this copy was made at a slightly later date than that at which the **FD** MS is generally thought to have been completed. Unlike most compositions for two lutes, both instruments play the bass line all through.

67. **D9** ff. 67v/68. "Wallsingham Jo Dowland". Diapason at D.
A ballad tune much used by composers for lute, virginals, viols, consorts, etc. In this setting Dowland elongates the tune to 12 bars, the more usual version consisting of 8 bars only. The original words have vanished, but Sir Walter Raleigh's poem, "As you came from the holy land, Of Walsingham" appears to be a rewriting of the old verses. When Ophelia sings the lines beginning "How should I your true love know" in *Hamlet*, Act IV, Sc. 5, she is quoting from the early ballad. The tune is used for Act I of "Mr Attowel's Jig" (*Shirburn Ballads*, Ed. A. Clark, 1907), the first verse of which appears to be a parody of a version of the Walsingham ballad. The tune was still known in the 18th century and was used by Gay in *The Beggar's Opera* in a version in common time.

68. **D5** ff. 38v/39. WT. "J.D.".
G ff. 21v/22. WT. Anon.
Tru f. 21 (modern numbering). "Aloe". The name presumably refers to the ballad "The

George Aloe". See Quiller-Couch *The Oxford Book of English Ballads* (1910), and Shakespeare (?) *The Two Noble Kinsmen*. Two of the verses sung by the Gaoler's Daughter in Act III, Sc. 5 of this play can, with some contrivance, be fitted to the tune.

Bar 10	2nd note	**Tru**	f on 4
11	beat 3 2nd q.	**Tru G**	g instead of f on 4
12	2 2nd q.	**Tru**	c on 1 repeated
	4 2nd q.		a on 1
21	4 2nd q.	**G**	c instead of b on 3
30	1 & 2	**Tru**	= ♪ ♪ ♪ ♪ ♪
34	4		a instead of c on 5
35	3		c on 6 added
	4		a on 6 added
48	2 2nd q.		c on 4 omitted
49	4 2nd q.		g on 4 omitted
			Last 8 bars omitted

69. **D9** ff. 68v/69/69v. "Loth to departe Jo: Dowland". Diapason at D.
There is a greater variety within the group of pieces called "Loth to depart" than in most of the other ballad and popular tunes. Nothing is known of the original words.

70. **D9** ff. 29v/30. "Robin Jo Dowland".
JP f. 22v. "Sweet Robyne". Anon.
JP f. 35. "Sweet Robyhn". Anon.
These two copies are almost identical, but each contains a number of small errors and discrepancies.
TGG pp. 114/115. "Galliarda JD". Diapason at D.
An extremely inaccurate version. A number of bars have been introduced which are in neither **D9** nor **JP**.
One of the most popular of all ballad tunes, it was set in many different versions for lute, bandora, virginals, viols and other combinations of instruments. It is called variously "Robin", "Sweet Robin", "Bonny Sweet Robin", "My Robin is to the greenwood gone", "Robin Hood is to the greenwood gone", "Bonn well Robin" (a variant form), and in **K10** "Schön wöhn ich gern etc". Ballads to the tune are found in the Roxburgh Collection and *The Crown Garden of Golden Roses* (1662). It survived into the 18th century and appears in A. Stuart's *Music for the Tea Table Miscellany* (1725) to the words "There Nancy's to the greenwood gone". The original words are no longer extant, but it is probably from these that Ophelia quotes (Hamlet, Act IV, Sc. 5) "For bonny sweet Robin is all my joy".

Bar 1	beat 3	**JP** 22v 35	a on 3 and c on 5 omitted
9	1	22v	c on 1, c on 2, e on 3, f on 4
Bar 9	beat 1 2nd q.	22v	a on 5, c on 6
13	3 2nd q.	35	a on 1 added
15	3	22v	e on 4 added
21	3 2nd q.	22v 35	a on 1 added
23	3	22v 35	e on 3 omitted, but added on 2nd half of the beat
34	1	22v	♪ ♪
34	1	35	♪ ♪
36	3	22v 35	= ♪ ; a on 2. The

			following e on 3 omitted
50	3 2nd q.	35	d on 2
51	3 2nd q.	22v 35	h on 6; a better reading
61	1	35	♪ ♪ ♪ ♩
64		22v 35	
71	3	22v 35	

COMPOSITIONS OF UNCERTAIN ASCRIPTION

71. **JP** f. 23v/24. "A Fantasia". Anon. Diapason at D.

This work shares so many of the characteristics of Dowland's other chromatic fantasies that it is tempting to ascribe it to him although a copy appears in J. D. Mylius *Thesaurus Gratiarum* (Frankfurt, 1622) which bears the rubric "Grammatica Rosideri Angli generosi". Sigmar Saltzburg, who kindly drew the editors' attention to this, suggests the possibility that the composer indicated was Rossiter. The composition is entirely out of style with other works by Rossiter and, in any case, it would not be the first time that an incorrect ascription was made to an English composer in a continental collection.

72. **G** ff. 42v/43. WT. Anon. Diapason at D.
The use of the descending chromatic hexachord and the general style suggest Dowland as the composer, but there are some features that are not entirely characteristic.

73. **D9** ff. 44v/45/45v. WT. Anon. Diapason at D.
The initial theme bears a strong resemblance to the tune "All in a garden Green", see **FVB** No. CIV by Byrd and **BD** p. 56 for Lyra Viol, Anon.
Several favourite devices of Dowland's are found in this piece, notably the use of little upward scales with the first note repeated and the use of many times alternated tonic-and-dominant harmony in approaching the final cadence. (*See* the final bars of both No. 2 and No. 9). No. 2 immediately precedes this piece in the MS and is also WT. and Anon. The text is in a state of confusion with regard to the placing of the bar lines. A crotchet value appears to have been lost immediately preceding bar 20, at the beginning of which the bar line is correctly placed. Following bar 36 an unlikely third repetition of the same phrase has been removed.

74. **31** f. 24. WT. Anon. Diapason at D.
The use of the opening theme of No. 1 suggests that Dowland might be the composer, although this is by no means certain proof that he is. Other composers have also used the same theme, notably the unknown writer of Phantasia No. 83 in Elias Mertel's *Hortus Musicalis*

Novus (1615). The very skilful construction is typical of Dowland and the change into the minor which only moves back to the major for the final cadence is a device consistent with his musical thought.

75. **D2** f. 48. "A Dream". Anon.
H f. 3. WT. Anon.
The style of this piece strongly suggests Dowland as composer. It is written on the same folio and just above No. 48 "Lady Laiton's Almain". (The title is not given in this MS.) The end of the piece continues right to the edge of the page leaving no room for title or composer's name. The words "A Dream" are written on the lowest line of the stave of the last bar. After the almain Dowland's name is written. In looking at the page it can well bear the interpretation that the name was intended to refer to the two pieces. Richard Newton has pointed out that a consort part for the cittern in C.U.L. 14.24 fits exactly with the piece at present under discussion. The unusual form makes a random coincidence impossible and it is clear that they are two distinct versions of the same piece. In the cittern book the name is given as "Lady Leighton's Pauen". The juxtaposition on the same page of two pieces connected with Lady Leighton suggests they may well be by the same composer. On the other hand it must be said that in **H** the piece occurs in a part of the MS where no authentic Dowland is found.

Bar 15   **H**

76. **G** f. 42. WT. Anon. Diapason at D.
D9 f. 19v. "Galliard". Anon. Diapason at D.
The opening phrase is the same as that of No. 19, and many of Dowland's characteristics of composition are present. In addition to the stylistic indications the position in **G**, between Nos. 3 and 72 points to Dowland as composer. In **D9** following the word "galliard" there is a contraction or mnemonic which appears to be "W th".

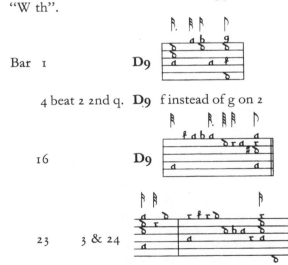

Bar 1   **D9**

4 beat 2 2nd q.   **D9**   f instead of g on 2

16   **D9**

23   3 & 24

77. **Mar** p. 382. "Mistris Norrishis Delight". Anon. Diapason at D.
There is no other evidence beyond the character of the piece to support a claim to Dowland as composer, but its rather unusual and spirited

tune suggests it might be his.

78. **G** f. 26. WT. Anon.

Its position in the MS suggests that this piece is by Dowland. It occurs in a group which contains some of his best known pieces; six precede it and three more follow, all without title or composer's name.

The general character, with its underlying melancholy, has much in common with No. 59.

79. **FD** f. 23. WT. Anon.

The first 18 bars of this setting of "What if a day" are undoubtedly in Dowland's handwriting. In the 19th bar the d of the first chord is written in the same hand, but for the b and a another quill has been taken up and is used to complete the piece. The appearance of the tablature is slightly altered but still remains very similar to Dowland's. Possibly this section of writing was added at a different time. Nevertheless the slight discrepancy in some of the letters could indicate another scribe. The fact that there are errors in the time values of bars 21, 22 and 23 would not preclude Dowland's having written the final six bars since his tablature on ff. 22v and 23v also contains some mistakes. The setting itself is typical of Dowland's treatment of popular and ballad tunes with its occasional departures from the more usual form.

80. **Myn** f. 7. "A Coye Joye". Anon.

This bears a strong resemblance to No. 57. Possibly an early version. As in most pieces in **Myn** the time marks are very unreliable. They have been corrected without further notice.

81. **D2** f. 56. WT. Anon.

Title from the Cambridge Consort Books where it is called "Tarletons Jigge". Dd.5.21 f. 5 (Recorder); Dd.3.18 f. 53 (Lute); Dd.5.20 f. 5 (Bass viol); Dd.14.24 f. 17 (Cittern). In Dd.4.23 f. 25 there is a solo Cittern version called "Tarletons Willy". The style is extremely reminiscent of Dowland's other jigs and the title of No. 59 suggests he had some connection with the famous comic actor. Possibly the tune was associated with the jig mentioned on the title-page of *News out of Purgatory*.

82. **D9** ff. 22/21v. WT.

The names "Dowland" and "F. Cutting" are both written at the bottom of this piece. In the opinion of the editors it is more consistent with Cutting's style than with that of Dowland.

83. **Myn** f. 12v. "Dowlands Galliard". Diapason at D.

W f. 15v/16. "My Lady Mildmays delighte". Anon. Diapason at D.

FD f. 22. "Johnsons gallyard". Diapason at D.

N6 f. 11. "Galliard Ro Johnson". Diapason at D.

38 f. 16v. "Mr Johnsons gallyard". Diapason at D.

Of these sources **FD, Myn** and **W** all date from about 1600. If Robert Johnson is the composer he must have written the piece before the age of about 17, since he was born *c*.1583. Young according to today's standards but not to the Elizabethans who matured early. It is significant that Dowland, though he added his name to six pieces and wrote others in his own hand in **FD**, did not claim this galliard by adding his signature. The weight of evidence seems entirely in Johnson's favour and the style is nearer Johnson's than Dowland's.

84. **D9** f. 17. "Hasellwoods Galliard Jo Dowland". **H** f. 3. WT. Anon.

This is No. 12, "Galliard", in Anthony Holborne's *Pavans, Galliards, Almains, etc.* (1599), in five parts. There is no reason to doubt that Holborne is the original composer. If Dowland is connected in any way with this piece it can only be as arranger for the lute. In the lute version the original composition is treated with little respect and the harmony is often changed for no apparent reason. The copy in **H** is very inaccurate; the divisions are undistinguished and the bass is frequently inconsistent with the bass of the statement. In all, the evidence suggests, unless these two versions happen to be exceedingly poor copies, that Dowland was responsible for neither, and that Holmes was mistaken in attaching his name to the piece.

85. **L** p. 218. "Galliarda Dulandi 39".

L p. 234. "Galiarda".

This is a rather poor version of a piece which, in other MSS, is ascribed to several different composers:

D2 f. 71v. "f Cuttings galliard".

31 f. 34. "a galiard by mr Cuttinge".

Mar p. 386. "Galliard Alfonsus".

G f. 29. WT. Anon.

Thy f. 33. "Maister Hayls Galliard".

The German tablature, in which this MS is written, is exceedingly inaccurate, and it can safely be assumed that most of the compositions are far from representing the original intention of the composer. Possibly they were written down from a not altogether reliable memory. In this and the next two pieces, in order to avoid the complexities of the German tablature, the French system has been substituted.

In the following bars the more general reading, with some slight variants among the four other versions, is as follows:

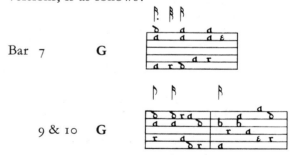

Bar 7   G

9 & 10   G

86. **L** p. 115. "Pauana Dulandi". Diapasons at F and D.

87. **L** p. 194. "Galliarda Dulandi 8". Diapason at F.

This is certainly not a galliard—possibly a setting of a chorale or psalm tune, but it is not recognisable as any of those that Dowland is known to have written or arranged. The last six bars hardly seem to belong to the earlier sections of the piece.

88. **30** ff. 3v/4. "The galliard to the pauan before". It is immediately preceded by "Pipers Pauan by John Dowlande B.M.". Diapason at D.

D9 f. 73v. WT. Anon. Diapason at D.

The same piece with some variant readings, and lacking the final four bars.

In the opinion of the editors this is not a genuine Dowland version. Many of the pieces in **30** bear traces of a personal handling. Possibly the writer of this MS had a taste for introducing variants of his own, or perhaps he had them from some other musician with this idiosyncrasy, from whom Holmes also had his copy of this piece. An example of this individualistic treatment is the two-part figure in bars 29, 30 and 31, which is not found in any well authenticated copies of this galliard but occurs again in the anonymous "Can she excuse" on f. 48 of the same MS. Daniel Bacheler makes great play with an exactly similar figure in his setting of "Mounsiers Almaine" in **Var.**

89. **30** f. 48. WT. Anon. Diapason at D.
For reasons against accepting this as an authentic Dowland version, see Note to 88. The first few bars closely resemble the "Gall: Mr D:B:" (Daniel Bacheler) of **LHC** f. 55, although the two pieces diverge in the later treatment and the **LHC** setting lacks the two-part figure already mentioned. The four-fold repetition of strain three in Bacheler's setting is extremely unusual if not unique.

90. **30** f. 42v/43. "Frogg galliard". Anon. Diapason at D.
This is another of the very personal settings in **30**. It is curious in that the first three bars correspond, with minor differences, to bars 9, 10 and 11 of No. 23a. In the first repeat (bars 17–33) an extra bar is introduced.

91. **D2** f. 52. "Suzanna Galliard". Anon.
Comparison with No. 38 shows this galliard to be almost certainly by Dowland, but in copying it Holmes has made a number of errors.

92. **D5** f. 63. "A Galliard fr. Cuttinge". Diapason at D.
As these notes will have already shown many lutenist composers, both English and Continental, adopted Dowland's themes and from them made compositions of their own. This setting is included as a matter of interest and as an example of the successful marriage of Dowland's melody (No. 24) with Cutting's style.

THE SCHELE LUTE MS. Hamburg Staats- und Universitätsbibliothek MB/2768
(Formerly Real. ND. VI, No. 3238)
On the fly-leaf Ernst Schele has inscribed the words Tablatur Buch and under them, he has added *Musica & vinum lætificant cor hominis*. His signature and the date, Anno 1619, are placed in the lower right hand corner.

In many cases the name of the city where the composition was collected by Schele, and the date, are added after the title and the composer's name. The earliest date given is 12 June 1613, and the latest, 23 Sept. 1616, but the dated pieces are not placed in chronological order. Among the towns mentioned are Paris, Metz, Frankfurt, Leyden and Naples.
This MS contains three long compositions attributed to Dowland, but which, in the opinion of the editors are as they stand, of dubious authenticity. The tuning of the lowest diapason at C in the first two of the three pieces would suggest that they late compositions, and yet they are in striking

contrast to the pieces in the Margaret Board Lute Book. In the case of No. 3 the attribution is borne out by 'Pauan' No. XI a 5, Thomas Simpson's *Opusculum* (1610), but the divisions seem lacking in the characteristics of Dowland's writing. The editors are grateful to Peter Holman for pointing out the identity of this piece with the *Opusculum* pavan, and also for calling their attention to the fact that No. 93 is a set of free variations on the *chanson* 'Une jeune fillette'. The treatment of this and whole of No. 94 again seem totally lacking in the stamp of his genius. Unfortunately the MS abounds in scribal errors and the editors have been obliged to make many corrections.

93. "Del Excellentissimo Musico Jano Dulando. Andegavi, Anno 1614. 22 Jun." pp. 25/26/27/28. Diapasons at F and C. The theme is a version of the popular—probably originally folk melody—known variously as "Madre non mi fa monaca", as "La Monaca" or "Une jeune fillette". The English version "The Queen's Almaine" appears in MSS for lute, bandora and cittern, besides Byrd's composition in the **FVB** (No. CLXXII).
The melody appears in a number of compositions from the late sixteenth and early seventeenth centuries. Eustache du Caurroy wrote no less than five instrumental fantasias on the theme. Arrangements for the lute are found in the following sources: **BTH** "Allemande Une jeune fillette" ff. 131v/132; **BNP** "Une jeune fillette" for three lutes and two viols, No. 4; **SdM** "Une jeune fillette a 9" pp. 43/44 (*Oeuvre de Nicolas Vallet*. **CNRS,** Paris, 1970, pp. 96–109); **JP** WT Anon. f.30v; **LHC** "Une jeune fillette Daniel", f.23v. Later the melody became associated with the text *Von Gott will ich nicht lassen,* and in this form was set as a chorale by J. S. Bach. For further information see John Wendland in *Acta Musicologica* Vol. XLVIII, 1976, Fasc. II. The writing of the variations seems particularly unconvincing as coming from Dowland. Note, for example, bars 169 to 172.

94. "Pauana Johan Douland" pp. 28/29/30/31. Diapasons at F, E♭ and C. The three strains consist of 19, 18 and 19 bars, each with its repeat. Although Dowland often departed from the traditional eight-bar strain of the pavan, in none of his other compositions in this form does he use so unconventional a construction as this.

95. "La mia Barbara. Johan Doulande Bacheler." pp. 49/50/51. Diapasons at F and D. The three are the same as those of "Pauan", No. XI a 5, in Thomas Simpson's *Opusculum* (1610), where it is attributed to Dowland. It is followed in this source by a galliard on the same theme by Simpson. With the title "Paduana Paul Sifert" it also appears in a setting for keyboard in Uppsala University Library, Instr. Mus. Ms 408, ff. 5v–7. (See *Lied und Tanzvariationen,* ed. W. Breig. Schott 6030, No. 4). Thanks are due to Peter Holman for pointing out this fact. Even if Dowland were the composer of the original strains it seems likely that the divisions are from another hand, possibly that of Schele himself.

THE MARGARET BOARD LUTE BOOK. In the possession of Robert Spencer.
In his notes to the Scolar Press facsimile edition (1976) Robert Spencer suggests that the compiler

of the MS was the daughter of Ninian Boord of Paxhill, Lindfield, Sussex, who married Henry Borne sometime between 1623 and 1631.

To judge by the level of technical skill demanded by much of the music, Margaret Board must have been a player of considerable ability. From the presence of a composition on f. 12v entitled "Almande Ro. Dowlande" in a hand which agrees in all details with that of John's own tablature script and some elementary instructions on one of the fly leaves also in his hand, it might even be inferred that she had received a lesson, or lessons from the great composer himself.

Four pieces, Nos. 96, 98, 99 and 100 in the present edition, are unique to this MS, while No. 97, which had previously made an anonymous appearance, is here credited to Dowland. There seems no reason to doubt the ascriptions even though two forms, the preludium and coranto, had not been used by him previously. In the case of the coranto he would have been following a fashion which began to show itself in the early years of the seventeenth century, and which, with many composers, especially in France, developed into an almost obsessive pre-occupation. The use of the term "Doctor" in the title of this piece suggests it must have been copied by Margaret Board during or after the year 1621.

96. An Almand By Mr. Jo: Dowland:
     Bacheler of Musique   f.13
97. The Queenes gall By Mr. Dowland
     Bacheler of Musique (D2 f.62,
     "Galliard" Anon.)   f.24
98. Preludium   f.29
99. Mr. Dowlands Midnight   f.26
100. Coranto By Doctor Dowland   f.30

On f.32v the following table of ornament signs appears:

ꜱ a pull back
(a fall forward
x to beat down the finger with a shake
: three pricks to be struck upwards with one finger
♯ for a long shake
c for a slide

These signs, however, do not appear to be applicable to the compositions on the folios preceding the table, but to those following it; they cannot, therefore, be taken as referring to the pieces by Dowland. No explanation of the single dot before a letter is given, but if the placing of this sign is compared with the ornamention of, for example, the versions of 'The King of Denmark's Galliard' in FD and 38, it will be found to coincide with notes on which it would be appropriate to place a 'pull back' or 'back fall', or in some cases, a short trill. The small cross x, does not appear to agree with the explanation given, and more probably indicates an ornament involving the note below the main one: a 'fore fall', a mordent, or even the ornament which goes by many different names, but consists of the notes of a major or minor third rising to the main note.

THE HAINHOFER MS, Wolfenbüttel.
101. Dritter Thail, f. 17, "Phantasia. Dooland."
102. Dritter Thail, f. 17, "Praeambulum. Doolant."
103. Sechter Thail, f. 6v, "Gagliarda. Dooland."
These three pieces, though possibly derived from compositions by Dowland, are hardly convincing in the form in which they appear in this MS.

NEW TO THE THIRD EDITION

104. H f.7. Anon. WT. This galliard was identified by John Ward from Matthew Otley's Cittern Book, now in his possession, where it appears as 'Ga.7/ Dowland per Ro[bert] Sp[rignell.] A version, without divisions, in D2, f. 41, and a setting for bandora in D2 f. 44, are also anonymous. The H f.7 copy was chosen for inclusion here since it has divisions, although these are not necessarily by Dowland.

105. Nür f. 4v. "Galliarda Douland Cantus." This also was found by John Ward. It is related to Dowland's "A galliard on a galliard by Daniel Bacheler", No. 28. In places it seems curiously incomplete and it is possibly one part of a setting for two or more lutes.

A composition in K10 f. 92v called "pavana dullande" is in fact by Tobias Kün, and can be found in TGG p. 62 called "Pavana Septima". It follows immediately after a setting of "Lachrimæ" by Valentinus Strobelius, and above the first line of tablature has the rubric "Respondens Lachrimæ". Hence presumably, Montbuisson's mistake.

ADDITIONAL SOURCES FOR SOME COMPOSITIONS

1. FANTASIA. Brahe f. 18v/22, "Fuga". A simplified version.
2. FORLORNE HOPE FANCY. Lvov ff. 54v/56, "fantasia", Anon.
3. FAREWELL. Mylius p. 1, "Grammatica illustris Douland"; TGG p. 18, "Fantasia 6", Anon.; Lvov ff. 41v/43, "Fantasia", Anon.
6. A FANCY. Mylius p. 18, "Fantasia 1", Anon.; Lvov ff. 39v/41, "Fantasi", Anon.
8. PIPER'S PAVAN. Linz f. 21, "Pauane", Anon. Eys f. 57, "Quis vis ingenius", Anon. (keyboard).
9. SEMPER DOWLAND SEMPER DOLENS. Prague, National Museum, MS IV. G. 18 ff. 38v/40, "Pauana Douland", Italian tablature.
10. SOLUS CUM SOLA. Board ff. 10v/11, "Solus cum sola by Mr Dowland Bacheler of Music"; L pp. 104/105, "Pauana 17", Anon.
15. LACHRIMAE. Board ff. 11v/12, "Lachrimæ J:D:"; Linz f. 11, "Pauana Lachrimi", Anon.; L pp. 122/123, "Pauana La Crumæ", Anon. Derived from "Lachrimæ" but with altered bass. Eys f. 24v, "Pavana Lachrima", Anon.
19. PIPER'S GALLIARD. Board f. 21v, "Yf my Complaynts Jo: Dowla B: M"; Dol ff. 92v/93, "Galliarde", Anon.; Matthew Otley's Cittern Book, f. [14], "Dowlands Gal"; CCB e. f.4v, "Piper's Galliard", Jo: Dowland/"Thomas Robinson". Different from NCL No. 9.
22. DOWLAND'S FIRST GALLIARD. Board 22v, "A Galliard", Anon. CCB e. f.28, "Galliarda Jo. Dowl".
23. THE FROG GALLIARD. Sch pp. 144/145, "Frogge Galliard", Anon. For 6 course lute. This elaborate setting has divisions unlike those of any other known copy, although the statement of each strain is closely related to Dowland's own version. Brahe ff. [6v/7], "Galiarda the frog", Anon.; Linz f. 94v, "Frogges Galliard", Anon. (German keyboard tablature.) L p. 198, "Rechenbergers Galliardt 15", Anon. L p. 230, "Galliarda I.A.F."; Nür f.13v, "Galliarda", Anon.

28. A GALLIARD ON A GALLIARD BY DANIEL BACHELER. **Board** ff. 16v/17, "Galliard D:B: A Galliard By Mr Jo: Dowland Bacheler of Museque".

40. THE KING OF DENMARK'S GALLIARD. **Board** ff. 17v/18, "The kinge of Denmark his gall", Anon. The following 25 bars have been added, whether by Dowland or not is uncertain:

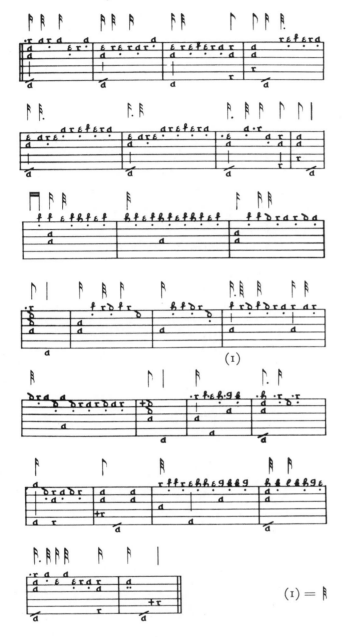

(1)

(1) = ♭

This section is followed by 44 bars with the title "Mr. Dowland his Battle gally". Apparently another version of the same piece. **Brahe** f. 24, "Galiarda Englese", Anon. A very simplified version.

41. QUEEN ELIZABETH'S GALLIARD. **CCB** e. f.8, WT, Anon.

42. CAN SHE EXCUSE. **Linz** f.41, "Galliarda Englessa", Anon.; **Flo** f.99, "Galiarda", Anon.; **Hain** Sechter Thail, f.22v, "Gagliarda Inglese Bella: Joan Dooland"; **B** f.293, "Galliarda Gregorii"; **B** f. 239v, "Galliarda", Anon. **Nür** f.6v, "Galliard Pipers No. 1" has the words "basslauten clause" written at the end. Possibly part of a duet. **Nür** f.7v, "Pipers Galliard No. 3", Anon.; **Nür** 66, "Aliter". **Eys** f.62v, "Galliard", Anon. (keyboard). EXCUSE ME. **NCL** No. 21, "Excuse me", Anon.

For many settings of this piece in country dance form, and its use in ballad operas until 1767, see John Ward, "A Dowland Miscellany". p. 67.

43. LADY RICH'S GALLIARD. **Sch** pp. 146–147, "My Lady Riches Galliard", Anon. For 6 course lute. This arrangement has elaborate divisions, apparently unique to this volume. **Brahe** ff. 16v/17, "Galliarda Englese", Anon. A very simplified version. **L** p. 145, "Intrada 6", Anon. **L** p. 190, "Galliarda 2", Anon.

44. EARL OF DERBY'S GALLIARD. **Sch** p. 142 "Mylord of Darbies Galliard. M. Johan Doulandt." Closely resembles **Var.** Galliard 4.

47. SMITH'S ALMAIN. **Brahe** (7v/8), "Balletto", Anon. **BD** p. 7, WT, Anon. An arrangement apparently based on Dowland, but neither strain is identical.

47a. SMYTHES ALLMAYNE. **Sch.** p. 148. "Almande". Anon. With the exception of a few mistakes and some minor differences of reading, identical with 38 f. 8v.

48. LADY LAITON'S ALMAIN. **Linz** f. 28, "Allemannd Doolannd Englessa"; **L** p. 498, "Anglicum", Anon. **CCB** b f. 28v, "Dowlands Allmaine"; *Matthew Otley Cittern Book*, ff. [13v/14], "Doulan: Gallia:", "Doulandes Galliarde".

48a. LADY LAITON'S ALMAIN. **Sch** p. 145, "Allmande Doulant". Almost identical with **FD** f. 48, but a bass has been added.

49. AN ALMAIN. **L** p. 479, "Almaine Engleiso", Anon.

50. MRS. WHITE'S THING. **Fab** f. 10v, "Mein hertz mit schmertz"; ff. 11/11v, "Ein schon Liedt Alio modo". Both arranged for lute. The second is followed by eight stanzas, each one beginning with a capital letter spelling the name MARGRETA. **CCB** e. f. 31, "Mrs. Whyte", Anon.

52. MRS. NICHOLS ALMAIN. **FM** II, No. 115, "Entrata", Anon. **L** p. 296, "Ballet 17", Anon.; **L** p. 448, "Sieh hertallerliebsters bild", Anon.; **Eys** f. 10, "Allamand" (keyboard).

60. COME AWAY. *Matthew Otley Cittern Book*, f. 11, "All the day", Anon.

61. ORLANDO. **Board** f. 1, "Orlando", Anon. Divisions to each strain.

62. FORTUNE. **Linz** f.34 "Fortune Dolland" (incomplete); f. 38, "Fortune Dollanndt".

63. COMPLAINT. **CCB** e. f.23, "Complainte", J. Dowlands"; **CCB** b. f.21v, "Complaint att ffortune" (cittern); **CCB** c. f.5, "Complainte" (recorder); **CCB** d. f.5, "Complainte" (bass viol).

69. LOTH TO DEPART. **Bro**, f. 92v.

85. GALLIARDA DULANDI 39. **27** f. 7. Third strain only.

For further additional sources, especially keyboard, see John Ward, "A Dowland Miscellany", *Journal of the Lute Society of America*, Vol. X, 1977.

In addition to the acknowledgements already made the editors would like to thank Dr. Howard Ferguson, Dr. Josef Klima, Mijndert Jape, Timothy Crawford and Robert Spencer for their valuable help in correcting misprints in the original edition, and also for providing information about additional sources for some of the compositions. They would also like to offer special thanks to Prof. John Ward for the generous help he has given in every way.

INDEX OF TITLES